Warrior • 106

D1028644

US Marine in Iraq: Operation *Iraq Freedom*, 2003

Richard S Lowry • Illustrated by Howard Gerrard

First published in Great Britain in 2006 by Osprey Publishing, Midland House, West Way, Botley, Oxford OX2 0PH, UK
443 Park Avenue South, New York, NY 10016, USA
E-mail: info@ospreypublishing.com

A CIP catalog record for this book is available from the British Library

ISBN 10: 1 84176 982 7
ISBN 13: 978 1 84176 982 0

Page layout by: Ken Vail Graphic Design, Cambridge, UK
Typeset in Helvetica Neue and ITC New Baskerville
Index by Alan Thatcher
Originated by United Graphics, Singapore
Printed in China through World Print Ltd.

06 07 08 09 10   10 9 8 7 6 5 4 3 2 1

FOR A CATALOG OF ALL BOOKS PUBLISHED BY OSPREY MILITARY AND AVIATION PLEASE CONTACT:

NORTH AMERICA
Osprey Direct, c/o Random House Distribution Center, 400 Hahn Road, Westminster, MD 21157
E-mail: info@ospreydirect.com

ALL OTHER REGIONS
Osprey Direct UK, P.O. Box 140 Wellingborough, Northants, NN8 2FA, UK
E-mail: info@ospreydirect.co.uk

www.ospreypublishing.com

Author's acknowledgments

I would like to thank Joanna de Vries for her unending patience and support throughout the development of this book. Thank you to Capt. Harold Qualkinbush USMC, Capt. James Reid USMC, Gunner David Dunfee USMC, Gunnery Sergeant Joe Muccia USMC and Cpl. Will Bachmann for their photographic contributions to this project. I would also like to thank Joe Raedle and Getty Images for supplying some of the most dramatic photographs of the war. Most of all, I would like to thank my wife Vickye; without her love and support none of this would have been possible.

Author's note

Troy Duncan and Terrell Johnson are fictitious characters. All other characters in this story are real: their real names are used, and the accounts of their actions are accurate. Duncan and Johnson are composite characters. In the first few chapters their stories are typical of everyday Marines, but during the actual battle, all of their experiences are those of actual Marines who fought in An Nasiriyah. I used Duncan and Johnson to tell the stories of Marines who might not otherwise have been mentioned, including Cpl. Will Bachmann, L/Cpl. Donald Cline, L/Cpl. Matthew Juska, Cpl. John Friend and several others.

I was extremely grateful for the opportunity to interview the following about their experiences:
Cpl. Will Bachmann, Capt. Michael Brooks, Cpl. Nicolas Elliot, HN Luis Fonseca (USN), LtCol. Rickey Grabowski, Maj. Bill Peeples, 1st Lt. James Reid, SSgt. William Schaefer, SSgt. Troy Schielein, Capt. Tod Schroeder, and Capt. Daniel Wittnam.

Dedication

This book is dedicated to the men and women of the United States Marine Corps who have chosen a life of service to their country.
Semper Fidelis
Richard S. Lowry

Artist's note

Readers may care to note that the original paintings from which the color plates in this book were prepared are available for private sale. All reproduction copyright whatsoever is retained by the Publishers. All inquiries should be addressed to:

Howard Gerrard,
11 Oaks Road,
Tenterden,
Kent,
TN30 6RD,
UK

The Publishers regret that they can enter into no correspondence upon this matter.

Editor's note

Unless otherwise stated all images are courtesy of the Official Marine Corps website and have been stated as cleared for release.

CONTENTS

US MARINE IN IRAQ: OPERATION *IRAQI FREEDOM*, 2003

INTRODUCTION

"We are just ordinary guys with an extraordinary job."
Major Christopher Starling USMC, 2d Marine Regiment, 2004

US Marine in Iraq: Operation Iraqi Freedom, *2003* provides an insight into the 21st-century Marine Corps – America's bravest young people, fighting in an ancient land. It follows the story of two fictitious Marines, Troy Duncan and Terrell Johnson. While the characters are fictitious, their experiences are accurate and are a composite of true stories of real Marines who fought and died in the first major battle of Operation *Iraqi Freedom*, the battle of An Nasiriyah. Troy Duncan and Terrell Johnson are typical American teenage boys when they enlist in the Corps. They quickly become young men as they survive the rigors of recruit and infantry training – they become Marines. Once they have completed their initial training, the two young Marines are assigned to the 1st Battalion of the 2d Marine Regiment at Camp Lejeune, NC. After training, Duncan and Johnson deploy to Iraq with Camp Lejeune's 1st Battalion, 2d Marine Regiment, part of the 2d Marine Expeditionary Brigade (2d MEB).

The fertile strip of land that lies between the Tigris and Euphrates rivers is often called the "cradle of civilization," where man first developed agriculture and the written word. For centuries this area of the Middle East

LEFT **A Task Force Tarawa Marine scans the southern Iraqi desert, watching for any indication of trouble. (Courtesy of Joe Raedle/Getty Images)**

has been dominated by conflict. In 1980 Saddam Hussein took over control of the government in a ruthless grab for power. In 1981 he invaded Iran over the long-disputed access to the Persian Gulf through the Shat-al-Arab and the valuable oilfields on the eastern bank of the waterway. Iran and Iraq fought for nearly a decade to a stalemate, until in 1988 Saddam finally realized that his land grab was futile and signed an armistice with his Iranian enemies.

In the summer of 1990 he turned on a weaker neighbor: his Arab enemies in Kuwait. The United States and the United Nations (UN) Security Council condemned the invasion of Kuwait and demanded that Iraq withdraw its troops, issuing Resolution 660, and later Resolution 661, which placed economic sanctions on Iraq. The powers of the Western world became concerned that the invasion of Kuwait would escalate into an Iraqi invasion of Saudi Arabia (which borders Kuwait), and threaten the world's oil supply. President George H.W. Bush announced that the US and Allied forces would deploy in a "wholly defensive" mission to protect Saudi Arabia. Immediately, troops began pouring in from all over the world in an operation labeled *Desert Shield*. When Saddam refused to leave Kuwait, Operation *Desert Storm* opened with six weeks of bombing from the most powerful air force ever assembled. On February 23, 1991 Bush announced that Saddam Hussein's army had been driven from Kuwait and declared a ceasefire.

Despite his embarrassing defeat in 1991, Saddam Hussein clung on to power. After *Desert Storm* the United States, with Allied support, had temporarily derailed his efforts to strengthen his international position. They had crippled his infrastructure with only six weeks of bombing, and then decimated most of his military in the 100 hours of *Desert Storm*'s ground war. This military operation was followed by the United Nations' policy of maintaining sanctions that kept Saddam from reconstituting his military forces.

BELOW **A tank from Alpha Company, 8th Tanks sets up position in front of a painting of Saddam Hussein at the garrison of the Iraqi 23d Infantry Brigade just north of An Nasiriyah. (Photo courtesy of Joe Raedle/Getty Images)**

Saddam had been working for ten years to recapture his stranglehold on the people of Iraq and to beat the United Nations' sanctions. He and members of his government tried to bribe United Nations and government officials, as well as leaders of industry throughout the world to get around the sanctions. Money that was meant as aid for the Iraqi people was diverted to Saddam's personal projects. Food and medicine were confiscated, and then sold on the black market. Meanwhile, in contravention of the sanctions, Iraq continued to rebuild its military forces. All the while, internal dissent against the dictatorship was forbidden. Stories of Saddam's "henchmen" regularly murdering, raping, and torturing Iraqi civilians on a whim filled Western newspapers, promoting worldwide concern over breaches of human rights. Alongside these concerns were the constant controversies over the manufacture of alleged nuclear and biological weapons by the Saddam regime.

After his election in 2000, President George W. Bush was anxious to ensure that the United Nations maintained the sanctions against Saddam. The primary concern among the Bush administration and other world leaders was that if Saddam rebuilt his army, it was highly probable that he would attack Israel, and that the Israelis would respond. In the current tense climate, this could have thrown the entire Middle East into armed conflict. War in the Middle East would certainly slow the flow of oil to the entire industrialized world, which could devastate the world economy.

On September 11, 2001 the unthinkable happened. A number of terrorists from a movement called Al-Qaeda based in Afghanistan (and, some thought, Iraq) hijacked four planes, crashing two into the World Trade Center Towers, New York, and one into the Pentagon in Washington DC. This unprecedented and well-coordinated terrorist attack saw the deaths of 3,000 innocent civilians. The radical group claimed to act in the name of Islam and condemned the Western world. America and its way of life were placed under direct threat in one of the first "foreign" terrorist attacks on American soil. President Bush and his advisors declared that Saddam had to be dealt with as part of America's "War on Terror." So while troops were sent to Afghanistan to hunt down members of Al-Qaeda, the Pentagon was also ordered to plan for the invasion of Iraq.

American military strategists knew that Saddam's power was rooted in Baghdad. So they planned for a swift penetrating invasion that would quickly bring Allied forces to the gates of Baghdad – Operation *Iraqi Freedom*. Most of the planners thought that the real fight would be for the capital, and that the thrust to Baghdad and passage across Iraq's southern wasteland would be relatively free from attack. So the US Army's V Corps was ordered to race northwest through the Iraqi desert with the 3d Infantry Division in the lead. The United States Marines were commanded to charge up the middle to hold Iraqi units in place.

The Marines would send their 1st Marine Expeditionary Force (I MEF). I MEF was a small corps, including Camp Pendleton's 1st Marine Division, the British 1st Armoured Division, Camp Lejeune's 2d Marine Expeditionary Brigade (2d MEB), the 3d Marine Air Wing (3d MAW), and all their supporting logistical units. The three reinforced Regimental Combat Teams (RCTs) of the 1st Marine Division would lead the Marine charge to Baghdad, while the British 1st Armoured Division

secured Iraq's "second" city, Basrah. Camp Lejeune's 2d MEB was given the mission of keeping the supply routes clear behind the 1st Marine Division's attack.

Designated Amphibious Task Force-East (ATF-E), seven amphibious naval ships carried the Marines half way around the world. 2d MEB was the only "East Coast" unit attached to the "West Coast" I MEF. Once on the ground in Kuwait, all of 2d MEB's aircraft were reallocated to the 3d MAW. BGen. Natonski redesignated his remaining units as Task Force Tarawa in order to provide an independent identity for the Camp Lejeune Marines.

As fate would have it, 2d MEB's lone Regimental Combat Team, RCT-2, would lead the charge toward Baghdad, while the 1st Marine Division secured the southern Iraqi oilfields. Task Force Tarawa was ordered to move to the Euphrates River and to secure the bridges in and around the desert city of An Nasiriyah. This is primarily an account of the Marines of the 2d MEB and RCT-2 during their fight to secure An Nasiriyah.

The Marines of RCT-2 fought against a determined enemy composed of entrenched regular soldiers of the 11th Infantry Division, local militia, Ba'ath Party loyalists and fanatic Fedayeen fighters armed with AK-47s, RPGs, RPK machine guns, tanks, technicals, mortars, and artillery. It is impossible to tell how many Iraqis actually participated in the battle. At the first sign of trouble most Iraqis abandoned their uniforms, melted into the civilian population, and fought in civilian clothes. Estimates of enemy strength range from 2,000–5,000 armed Iraqis.

Task Force Tarawa Marines fought for a week to secure the bridges and routes through An Nasiriyah, while 1st Marine Division's three RCTs crossed the Euphrates River and proceeded north to their objective – Baghdad. US Marines and soldiers of the 3d Infantry Division arrived at the outskirts of Baghdad at nearly the same time. The 3d Infantry Division swept westward to the Saddam Airport, while the Marines moved into eastern Baghdad.

The invasion of Iraq began officially on March 20, 2003. Baghdad was formally secured by US forces on April 9, 2003, but was not completely cleared of conventional enemy forces until April 12. The statue of Saddam Hussein fell on April 9. On May 1, 2003 President George W. Bush announced the end of major combat operations in the Iraq War. However, US troops remained, and still remain in 2006, conducting stabilization operations and helping the Iraqis to rebuild their infrastructure.

CHRONOLOGY

January 6	2d Marine Expeditionary Brigade (2d MEB) formed.
January 16	Amphibious Task Force-East (ATF-E) and 2d MEB leave the North Carolina coast and begin their transatlantic journey to the Middle East.
January 28	ATF-E and 2d MEB cross the Straits of Gibraltar, entering the Mediterranean Sea.
February 1	ATF-E and 2d MEB transit the Suez Canal, entering the Red Sea.
February 4	ATF-E and 2d MEB transit the Bab el Mandeb Strait, entering the Gulf of Aden.
February 11	ATF-E and 2d MEB sail through the Straits of Hormuz, entering the Persian Gulf.
February 17	2d MEB, now named Task Force Tarawa (TFT), disembarks at Kuwaiti Naval Base and moves by air and land to Camps Shoup and Ryan in the northern Kuwaiti Desert.
March 9	TFT reports all of its units are combat ready.
March 19	TFT units begin movement to Assembly Area Hawkins in preparation for the invasion of Iraq.
March 20	The President of the United States announces the beginning of Operation *Iraqi Freedom*.
March 21	TFT units conduct breach operations and begin moving into Iraq.
March 22	RCT-2 arrives at Jalibah Airfield.
March 23	3d Battalion, 2d Marines secure western Euphrates River crossing for the 1st Marine Division movement to Baghdad.
March 23	US Army 507th Maintenance Company takes wrong turn and is attacked while moving through An Nasiriyah. Casualties number 11 soldiers killed and six taken prisoner.
March 23	1st Battalion, 2d Marines move to secure the eastern bridges in An Nasiriyah. Casualties number 18 Marines killed and dozens wounded.
March 24	2d Battalion, 8th Marines fight to maintain control of An Nasiriyah's eastern Euphrates River bridge, while lead elements of the 1st Marine Division brave Ambush Alley to push toward Baghdad.
March 25	3d Battalion, 2d Marines return to RCT-2 in southern An Nasiriyah to support 2d Battalion, 8th Marines' effort to defeat the enemy in the city and secure the highway leading to the eastern bridges.
April 2	An Nasiriyah declared secure, RCT-2 packs up and moves north.
April 10	TFT defeats remnants of the Iraqi 10th Armored Division and seizes Al Amarah.
April 11	TFT units secure Al Kut airfield.
May 18	2d MEB returns to the ships of ATF-E.
May 19	ATF-E and 2d MEB begin the voyage home.
June 24	Most of the sailors and Marines of 2d MEB return home to Camp Lejeune.
June 29	USS *Kearsarge* arrives off Carolina Coast, bringing the remaining sailors and Marines of 2d MEB home.

RECRUITMENT

A few good men

In Atlanta, Georgia, hidden in a rarely visited strip mall across from a popular shopping center, is a group of government offices. The windows are adorned with glamorous posters and military insignia. Two distinct groups of people frequent these offices: spit-and-polish soldiers, sailors, airmen, and Marines, each service vying for the attention of the young men and women in the second group.

Local teenage boys and girls are drawn here out of curiosity. Most are still in high school. Some have either graduated or dropped out. All are looking for a job or a way out of their current lives. Nine out of ten applicants to the Marine Corps fail to qualify, as the Marine recruitment policy favors high school graduates who have not had major problems with the law. The Marines are looking for intelligent young men and women who can become an asset to the Corps.

One of our composite characters, Troy Duncan, is a typical 19-year-old, first-year history major, who had just started college when the World Trade Center towers crumbled to the ground. He had entered college because he wanted to teach, but he was not sure if he belonged there when the planes struck. Duncan hardly slept that night. The images of those crumbling buildings had changed his life. Lying in bed with his eyes wide open, he stared at the ceiling for hours. By 3am, he knew what he had to do. Just as his father had done before him, and his father's father, he had to find a place to make his mark. He would join the Marines. There he knew he could make a difference.

By 6am on September 12, 2001, Duncan was waiting for the recruiting office to open. Around 6.30am, another young boy about Duncan's age sauntered up. Terrell Johnson, our other composite character, had come to the Marines for nearly the same reason as Troy Duncan. He wanted to do something positive with his life. Johnson had finished high school and started looking for work. He had tried working at Taco Bell for a few weeks. Then he found a job at the local Barnes & Noble – he loved books. Without saying a word, he sat down next to Duncan and pulled out a tattered copy of *Fight Club*, opened it and began to read.

By 8am, the line had grown to a half dozen young men. A new, nondescript car pulled up into the parking space at the front door labeled "Reserved USMC" and a Marine staff sergeant climbed out of the driver's seat. The sergeant was dressed in neatly pressed blue trousers with a red stripe running down the side of the legs, a khaki shirt and the distinctive white Marine Corps hat. He quickly ordered the boys into the office.

Duncan followed the staff sergeant to his desk and explained that he wanted to join the Marine Corps. The staff sergeant gave him the standard enlistment form, several pages long, full of questions like: "Have you ever used recreational drugs?" "Have you ever been convicted of a crime?" The Marine Corps has always sought to recruit the best of the best in the tradition of "the few, the proud," and it continues to do so, attracting young men and women from a broad spectrum of society. The Marine Corps is the youngest of all the American military services: the age of the average Marine is around 24 years, and there are nearly 19,000 teenagers in the Corps. After the initial questionnaire the next step for the potential Marines is the test. Duncan and Johnson both

RIGHT Two Marines recite
the Oath of Enlistment at a
Military Entrance and Processing
Station for Recruiting Station,
Springfield, MA. The ceremony
is a hallmark event for those
entering military service. (Photo
courtesy Staff Sergeant Jonathan
Agee. USMC)

passed and two weeks later returned to the parking lot, each armed with a small duffle bag.

Before arriving at the Marine Corps recruit training depot, Parris Island, SC, and beginning their lives as Marines the new recruits are officially sworn into the Corps, their first important experience of Marine tradition. The honor of this occasion is impressed upon them by their accompanying staff sergeants. A Marine officer leads the ceremony, asking them to "Raise your right hand and repeat after me:"

> I do solemnly swear (or affirm) that I will support and defend the Constitution of the United States against all enemies foreign and domestic; that I will bear true faith and allegiance to the same. That I will obey the orders of the President of the United States and the orders of the officers appointed over me, according to the regulations and the Uniform Code of Military Justice. So help me God.

RECRUIT TRAINING

Parris Island, South Carolina

When the new Marines are ushered off the bus at Parris Island, often bewildered and exhausted, they perform yet another lasting tradition. The Drill Instructor (DI) greets them as they get off the bus and orders them to line up, placing their feet on the four rows of 15 sets of yellow footprints that are painted in front of the Receiving Barracks Company. They are told to turn and look at the man beside them, who will be their "buddy" throughout the training process.

Parris Island takes in the recruits from the eastern half of the nation, while the Marine Corps Recruit Depot, San Diego, trains Marines on the west coast. The dividing line is the Mississippi River. Johnson, Duncan, and the other new recruits would spend the next 11 weeks being molded into Marines at Parris Island. They would be subjected to the Marine Corps' ethos for 24 hours a day. From the moment these young men and women stepped off the bus and planted their feet on the yellow footprints, they were being reshaped into United States Marines.

Duncan and Johnson, like all new recruits, spent the first few days of their 11 weeks of training drawing uniforms and equipment, undergoing physical and dental exams, having vaccinations and getting their first Marine haircut. On enlistment the Marine Corps provides its men and women with personal equipment, from their socks to their Kevlar helmets. At the start of their Marine career, recruits wear only their utility uniforms. These are the equivalent of the army's Battle Dress Uniforms (BDUs), except that the Marine utility uniform has a unique camouflage pattern and each one has the famous "Eagle, Globe, and Anchor" stenciled on the breast pocket.

The recruits were split up into 75-man platoons. There were enough new recruits to form four platoons. The four platoons were grouped in a "series." Each platoon was broken down into squads and, of course, every recruit had a buddy. The new Marines are quickly schooled in the Corps' structure.

Marine Enlisted Ranks

	ENLISTED RANK
E-1	Private
E-2	Private First Class
E-3	Lance Corporal
E-4	Corporal
E-5	Sergeant
E-6	Staff Sergeant
E-7	Gunnery Sergeant
E-8	First Sergeant/Master Sergeant
E-9	Sergeant Major/Master Gunnery Sergeant

Marine Officer Ranks

	OFFICER RANK
O-1	Second Lieutenant
O-2	First Lieutenant
O-3	Captain
O-4	Major
O-5	Lieutenant Colonel
O-6	Colonel
O-7	Brigadier General
O-8	Major General
O-9	Lieutenant General
O-10	General

In the weeks that followed, they would absorb the common tasks of military life. They would learn to march and talk like Marines. They would learn how to take care of themselves and their uniforms and equipment: and they would learn the basic skills needed in a Marine's daily life.

The recruits also received their first introduction to the "soul" of the Marine Corps when they undertook lessons in the Corps' core values – *Honor, Courage, and Commitment.* In the Corps these are not idly spoken words, they are a tradition and way of life. These values are engrained in every aspect of recruit training. Honesty and integrity are expected of

every recruit. They are taught that the only way to lose is to quit. They are conditioned with a regime of diet and exercise to turn them into physically fit warriors. They learn how to handle and care for their M16A2 rifle as if it were an extension of their body.

The platoon began learning marksmanship skills in the classroom, before being taken to the rifle range. Two platoons would fire in the morning, while the other two would "pull butts" (changing targets and keeping scores). Pulling butts was a more important part of the recruit training than it seemed at first: here, the recruits learned what it sounded like when they were being shot at. Each bullet, traveling faster than the speed of sound, generated a mini sonic boom. If you were close enough to the flying bullet, you could hear the distinctive crack of the passing projectile.

After rifle qualifications, the weeks flew by. The recruits underwent academic testing, drills, and inspections. On the next to last week of training, the recruits received Basic Warrior Training in which they learned fundamental field skills. They learned how to dig a fighting

position. They learned about personal hygiene and how to keep themselves and their equipment clean in the field. They learned how to read a map and navigate with a compass. Then they learned how to fast rope and finally they were sent to the gas chamber.

The gas chamber has been a part of each military service's recruit-training program for many years. While there is some value in training recruits in the proper procedure for donning a gas mask and a need to demonstrate the consequences of not properly seating it, the gas chamber "event" has become more a rite of passage than a training exercise. The recruits are taken into a block building, told to don their masks and then tear gas is set off in the closed room. Always, the recruits are ordered to remove their masks and then leave the gas-filled chamber in an orderly fashion.

The final week takes the recruits to the "Crucible." It is a severe test of patience and fortitude, and is the final trial of Marine Recruit Training. The Crucible emphasizes teamwork under stress. The recruits get eight hours of sleep during the entire 54-hour exercise. They march 40 miles in those 54 hours and receive two and a half MREs (Meals Ready to Eat), which they must ration to last the entire exercise. MREs are the US military's high-tech field meal, and have been specifically developed to provide the calories, vitamins, and nutrients required for troops fighting in the field. They are lightweight and packaged for extremely long shelf lives. The food is packaged in a tough plastic pouch that is actually aluminum foil and plastic layered together.

The Crucible is designed to test the recruits to their utmost and to teach them that it is together, rather than alone, that they are unstoppable.

ABOVE **During their school of infantry training Marines are taught vital fieldcraft skills, including how to navigate a grid coordinate. Here Marines at the School of Infantry are taking part in a vehicle land exercise to become more efficient in deployment environments. (Photo courtesy L/Cpl. Zachary R. Fran)**

It is a grueling mental and physical challenge that the recruits must pass to become Marines. Toward the end of their trial, Duncan and Johnson, like all their comrades, had never been so tired in their entire lives, but remained determined. With the end in sight, all the recruits were spurred on by a renewed energy. The drill instructors begin "Jody calls." Jody calls are a responsive cadence, named after a fictional character "Jody" whose luxurious lifestyle is contrasted with military deprivations. Jody is the person who stays at home, drives the Marine's car, and gets the Marine's sweetheart while the Marine is in recruit training. The exhausted recruits joined in:

> Way back when at the dawn of time.
> In the heart of Death Valley where the sun don't shine.
> The roughest toughest fighter ever known was made.
> From an M-16 and a live grenade.
> He was a lean mean green fighting machine.
> He proudly bore the title of US Marine.

By the time they reached the Parade Deck and the half-size replica of the famous Iwo Jima Memorial, Johnson, Duncan, and the others had marched over 40 miles in a little over two days. They were shouting out the cadence at the top of their lungs and marching in unison. The company stopped at the memorial and the men grounded their packs, placed their heavy Kevlar helmets on their packs and donned their caps. The colors were raised on the memorial and there was a short ceremony. The drill instructor presented each man with an Eagle, Globe and Anchor insignia, shook their hands and for the first time said, "Good work, Marine."

The last week was an anti-climax. The new Marines spent most of the time preparing to leave Parris Island. Most would return home for a short leave before they went to the School of Infantry. At the graduation ceremony, Johnson and Duncan not only emerged as Marines, but also as best friends. They both got orders to the School of Infantry at Camp Geiger, North Carolina.

School of Infantry – every Marine a rifleman

Parris Island had turned Duncan and Johnson into Marines but their training was far from complete. After a short leave they reported to the School of Infantry (SOI) at Camp Geiger, within the giant Marine Corps complex at Camp Lejeune, North Carolina. SOI would provide the transition from boot camp to the operating forces. Every year 18,000 Marines undergo realistic, aggressive, and safe training at SOI. The school turns them into Marine warriors.

The School of Infantry is broken down into two training battalions for entry-level Marines. Marines who will be assigned to the infantry report to the Infantry Training Battalion, while all other Marines are sent to the Marine Combat Training Battalion. No matter what their job in the Marine Corps, from public affairs, to motor transport mechanic, to supply clerk, every Marine is trained to be, first and foremost, a rifleman. "Every Marine a rifleman" is a time-honored concept that has set the Marines apart ever since the Corps' inception in 1775, when every man who volunteered was required to bring his own musket.

Duncan, Johnson, and all the Marines at SOI learned to become one with their rifle. They learned to live the creed first put forward by MGen. William H. Rupertus USMC soon after the Japanese attacked Pearl Harbor in December, 1941:

This is my rifle. There are many like it, but this one is mine. It is my life. I must master it as I must master my life. Without me my rifle is useless. Without my rifle, I am useless. I must fire my rifle true. I must shoot straighter than the enemy who is trying to kill me. I must shoot him before he shoots me. I will. My rifle and I know that what counts in war is not the rounds we fire, the noise of our burst, or the smoke we make. We know that it is the hits that count. We will hit. My rifle is human, even as I am human, because it is my life. Thus, I will learn it as a brother. I will learn its weaknesses, its strengths, its parts, its accessories, its sights and its barrel. I will keep my rifle clean and ready, even as I am clean and ready. We will become part of each other. Before God I swear this creed. My rifle and I are the defenders of my country. We are the masters of our enemy. We are the saviors of my life. So be it, until victory is America's and there is no enemy.

Every Marine, regardless of Military Occupational Specialty (MOS), is trained in common skills. Thus, both battalions conduct nearly identical training in the first several weeks. The training is designed to further engrain the Corps' core values of *Honor, Courage, and Commitment* into every new Marine and prepare him or her mentally, physically, and morally for the challenges of 21st-century warfare.

Johnson and Duncan reported in to student administration where they were assigned to their training unit. During the first days they were issued field gear from supply and a rifle from the armory. The first weeks were filled with common skills training. Duncan and Johnson spent many hours in the classroom and out in the field watching demonstrations, then repeating their newly learned skills. Every day had time set aside for Physical Training (PT). Slowly, but surely, their bodies were conditioned to the rigors of combat. They also learned the basics of being a Marine infantryman, and they discovered everything there was to know about their M16A2 rifle. They carried their rifles everywhere. The learned to take them apart, clean them, and put them back together – blindfolded. They became Marine Riflemen.

The US Army first fielded the M16 rifle during the Vietnam War, in the early 1960s. The initial shortcomings of the design were worked out over the next several years and an improved weapon, the M16A2, was first adopted by the Marine Corps in 1983. Marine infantryman have been carrying the M16A2 ever since. It is a lightweight, air-cooled, gas-operated, magazine-fed weapon designed for either three-round bursts or semi-automatic, single-shot fire. The rifle uses NATO standard 5.56mm ammunition carried in 30-round magazines. The weapon is accurate at ranges of up to 500 meters and has a maximum effective range of 800 meters.

They also learned how to use the other lethal tools of their trade. They learned how to operate the M203 grenade launcher, an attachment for their rifle that could hurl 40mm grenades more than 200 meters into

enemy positions. They were taught to throw standard grenades and fire light- and medium-weight machine guns. They learned how to shoot AT-4 and Shoulder-launched Multi-purpose Assault Weapon (SMAW) rockets, and how to set up and detonate Claymore mines. In addition to their weapons training, they studied basic map reading and land navigation skills, and were trained in basic radio operation.

Another important part of their modern-day training was lessons in nuclear, biological, and chemical (NBC) war-fighting skills. They learned how to don their Mission Oriented Protective Posture (MOPP) suits quickly and to continue fighting while wearing the bulky protective garments and gas masks. They also practiced firing their M16s while clad in their MOPP gear. A MOPP suit will protect the wearer from radioactive particles, chemical, and biological agents. It consists of heavy, charcoal-lined pants and a hooded jumper, heavy rubber gloves, and booties, as well as a gas mask which can filter tiny particles from the air. The entire suit is designed to be worn over the utility uniform and protective body armor. Once a Marine has donned his MOPP suit, he is completely encased in a protective outer layer of clothing, but the heavy garments hinder his ability to maneuver and fight on the battlefield. The Marine moves more slowly. His vision is hampered by the gas mask. It becomes difficult to communicate with others and shoot straight. The Marines hate the suit. They are hot, bulky, and uncomfortable. Psychologically, the very thought of needing to wear a MOPP suit into battle is frightening because every Marine knows what the suits are meant to protect against – nerve gas, biological agents, and radioactive materials.

The Marine students were taught basic offensive maneuvers and defensive tactics. They were taught how to conduct patrols and how to

move and fight in urban terrain. They learned how to handle enemy prisoners and the basics of battlefield first aid. All the while they continued their daily PT and physical conditioning, with martial arts training and regular 15km (9.3 miles) road marches.

Once they have completed their basic infantry training the Marines are split into groups according to their Military Occupational Specialty (MOS). All of the non-infantry Marine graduates had moved on to their specialized MOS training, but the infantrymen remained at Camp Geiger for another five weeks to conduct specific MOS training.

Marine Infantry Military Occupational Specialties

MOS	SPECIALTY	PROFIENCY
0311	Marine Rifleman	M16A2, SAW, M240 grenade launcher, and infantry tactics
0331	Machine Gunner	.50 cal. and 240G machine guns
0341	Mortarman	60mm and 81mm mortars
0351	Assaultman	SMAW and demolitions
0352	Antitank Guided Missileman	Javelin and TOW

They were then split up to undergo specialized training required in their particular infantry specialty. All of the combined skills would be needed within a Marine rifle company. Most Marines were assigned to 0311 training, Marine Rifleman. Others learned how to handle, maintain and employ the other weapons in a Marine rifle company.

The riflemen would receive even more advanced infantry training in tactics and weapons. They learned to fire and care for the M249 Squad Automatic Weapon (SAW). The machine gunners got advanced training on the maintenance and care of the 240G medium machine gun and the venerable .50 cal. machine gun. Antitank Guided Missilemen learned the intricacies of the TOW and newer Javelin missiles, and Mortarmen learned how to quickly set up and fire both the lightweight 60mm mortars and the heavier 81mm mortars used at the battalion level.

Both Johnson and Duncan wanted to be riflemen. By the time they graduated from SOI, they were mentally, physically, and morally prepared for the challenges of 21st-century warfare. and anxiously awaited their assignments. To their pleasant surprise, they were assigned to the same unit, both receiving orders to the 1st Battalion of the 2d Marine Regiment across the river from Camp Geiger, in Camp Lejeune.

Combined Arms Exercise, Twentynine Palms, California

Duncan and Johnson were now ready for assignment to an operational Marine infantry regiment. The 2d Marine Regiment existed in several different forms at the beginning of the 20th century. Portions of the 2d Marines served in China, the Philippines, Haiti, and Cuba. It was not until World War II that the regiment made history when it fought a determined enemy for control of a tiny coral atoll in the South Pacific, on Tarawa in 1943 – one of the bloodiest battles in Marine history. The 2d Marine Regiment suffered heavy casualties in one of the first large-scale amphibious landings in the Pacific campaign, thus earning the motto which they follow today, "Keep Moving." On Tarawa, their 3d Battalion pressed the attack through shallow waters and obstacle-strewn beaches to defeat the Japanese defenders, winning the title of the "Betio Bastards," a title that they proudly carry to this day.

The 2d Marine Regiment of the 21st century had become one of the finest fighting regiments of any military organization anywhere in the world. They had modern equipment, professional leadership, and more than 5,000 Marines trained in the traditions of the Marine Corps. The regiment had three infantry battalions and the support of 2d Tank Battalion, 2d Light Armored Reconnaissance Battalion, and 2d Assault Amphibian Battalion, not to mention their close ties with the 10th Marine Artillery Regiment at Camp Lejeune and the Marine aviators across the New River.

2d Marines' three infantry battalions each occupied facilities on three parallel roads within Camp Lejeune. Down the road from each battalion was the regimental headquarters. The modern Marine Corps' basic fighting unit is the infantry battalion. It is the building block from which all larger units are assembled. Seldom does an entire regiment deploy or fight as a complete entity.

Today, the Marine Expeditionary Unit (MEU) is deployed most often. The Marines developed MEUs and made them Special Operations Capable (MEU-SOC). Each MEU spent six-month deployments at sea aboard US Navy amphibious ships. Two MEUs were usually afloat at any one time. They were America's "911" force, able to respond to any worldwide emergency in a matter of days, and carrying everything they needed to cope with any contingency. The MEU's Ground Combat Element (GCE) was basically a Marine infantry battalion. They were supported by a platoon of AAVs (Assault Amphibian Vehicles), a platoon of tanks, LAVs (Light Armored Vehicles), and an artillery battery.

Each MEU also had an Air Combat Element (ACE), which contained a handful of just about every type of aircraft in the Corps' inventory. There were a few CH-46 Sea Knight and Huey helicopters, as well as a couple of CH-53 Sea Stallions to lift Marines ashore. There were some AH-1 Cobra Attack helicopters for close air support (CAS) and a few Harriers for deeper reconnaissance and heavier CAS missions.

The 2d Marine Regiment supplied its battalions to the MEU deployment schedules on a rotating basis. At the end of each deployment Marines are promoted, transferred, and some even finish their enlistments. Once they have taken some time off and some have transferred out, a new set of Marines are brought in to rebuild the battalion. Months are then spent rebuilding the newly formed battalion with a full training schedule. In 2002, the 2d Marine Regiment's battalions were each in a different phase of this staggered cycle. The 2d Battalion was in the middle of its building and training process. It would be the next to deploy with a MEU.

The 1st Battalion had just returned from an MEU deployment and they were in a reconstitution phase when Johnson and Duncan arrived. The core of 1/2d was its three rifle companies (Alpha, Bravo, and Charlie), each containing three infantry and one weapons platoon. The weapons platoon provided each company commander with some heavier weapons. They had 240G 7.62mm machine gun teams, a 60mm mortar section, as well as assault and sniper teams. Duncan and Johnson had both been assigned to the 3d Platoon of Charlie Company.

BELOW **1st Battalion, 2d Marines training in the Kuwaiti desert. On arrival in Kuwait the Marines conducted many training exercises to pull together their expertise and acquaint themselves with the type of terrain that they would be fighting in. This would be the last training opportunity before pushing off into Iraq. (Photo courtesy Gunner David Dunfee USMC)**

The commander of the 1st Battalion was a career Marine. He had risen through the enlisted ranks to staff sergeant and then left the Corps to get a college education. He returned as a second lieutenant and worked his way up from platoon leader to company commander, and then to battalion commander. He was an old-school Marine, a "Mustang." He lived for the Corps and spent every day of his life preparing to take his Marines into battle. A stoic leader who ran his battalion by the book, he cared for each and every one of his men, but never showed it.

When a commander first takes over a battalion, he has the privilege of selecting a call sign that he will use in all radio transmissions. LtCol. Rickey Grabowski had selected "Timberwolf" as his call sign. He felt that the daily lives of these predatory animals that traveled in packs closely resembled how Marines fight together. So, the entire battalion came to be known as the "Timberwolves." As the commanding officer, Grabowski held the designation of "Six." His intelligence officer, the S-2, was Timberwolf 2; the operations officer, the S-3, was Timberwolf 3, and so on. Timberwolf 6 knew he had the most important job in the Marine Corps – command of an infantry battalion.

More and more new faces showed up every day, and soon the Timberwolves were nearly back to full strength. The battalion commander scheduled training for every day. Charlie Company's commander took the time to get to know his Marines. Capt. Dan Wittnam was another "Mustang" who had risen through the enlisted ranks to become an officer. Duncan and Johnson respected him immediately. Wittnam was tough, yet fair. He took an interest in all of his men.

The lot of a peacetime Marine is to train, train, and then train some more. Duncan and Johnson's days were filled with classes, exercises, and PT. Soon the battalion staff began preparing for a Combined Arms Exercise (CAX), when the entire battalion could be pulled together into

RIGHT **Aboard the USS _Ponce_ on the way to war. Here the Marines are seen in their desert camouflage uniforms. Unlike the woodland camouflage pattern on their MOPP suits, these were designed to help them blend in with their combat environment. (Photo courtesy Gunner David Dunfee USMC)**

a coherent unit. The battalion would train as a mechanized infantry battalion. A Company of AAVs from 2d AAV Battalion, a company of tanks from 2d Tank Battalion and the 1st Battalion of the 10th Marine Artillery Regiment would support them in the exercise. In addition, the Regimental Command group would attend the exercise to practice their skills of fighting as a Regimental Combat Team (RCT).

An RCT is a Marine regiment fully equipped for combat. The regiment's three infantry battalions are usually supported by a battalion of artillery, and at least a company each of AAVs, LAVs and tanks. The RCT usually works with a complete Marine Air Group (MAG), consisting of a rotary wing lift squadron and an attack squadron producing a war-fighting Marine Air Ground Task Force (MAGTF). The RCT Command element planned to attend CAX with 1/2, and then they would rotate the "Betio Bastards" in to replace the Timberwolves in a "Super-CAX."

Everyone in the battalion and the regimental headquarters worked from dawn to dusk for nearly a week preparing to travel to the desert. Then on a cold Monday morning, the Timberwolves, along with the Marines in the regimental headquarters, loaded on to buses that would carry them to waiting aircraft for their day-long journey across the United States to the Marine Corps Air, Ground Combat Center (MCAGCC) in Twentynine Palms, California.

Hundreds of thousands of Marines have trained at the center near Twentynine Palms since its inception in 1952. The vast expanse of the base in the southern Californian desert is ideal for training and live-fire exercises. The terrain in the giant facility varies from flat wasteland, to rolling sandy desert, to mountains and valleys. Twentynine Palms is able to support regimental-size training exercises within its massive borders. The Marines maneuver and fire upon a fictitious enemy, Opposing Force (OPFOR), known throughout the Corps as the Mojavians.

CAX provides a 22-day, intense, live-fire, combined-arms training course. There are a series of progressive exercises, starting at company level and working up to a finale. All three of 1/2's infantry companies were

ABOVE **A Marine Light Armored Vehicle during CAX at Twentynine Palms, California. (Photo courtesy USMC)**

integrated with the AAV company. Each rifle platoon would ride in three AMTRACs or AAVP7 armored assault tracked amphibious vehicles.

The AAV, the latest version of Marine tracked landing craft, entered the Marine Corps in the early 1970s. It was designed to carry 25 Marines from ship to shore, providing protection from small arms fire and small pieces of shrapnel. Its aluminum alloy hull allowed movement through the water at up to 13kph (8mph) and road speeds of up to 72kph (45mph). While the light armor increased vehicle speed, it provided virtually no protection from larger caliber weapons.

The AAVP7 is equipped with a MK-19 automatic grenade launcher and a .50 cal. machine gun located in a small turret on the right front of the vehicle. The vehicle commander rides in the turret, or "up-gun" as it has come to be known. The up-gun can provide vehicle protection and suppressive fire in support of its infantry after they dismount. There is a large ramp in the rear of the vehicle which is dropped to load and dismount Marines and equipment. The roof of the troop compartment can also be opened, allowing Marine riflemen to stand on the benches and fire from within the track.

Duncan and Johnson did not like riding in the hot metal boxes. Their aluminum alloy hulls seemed to provide little protection, and the "tracks" seemed to be nothing more than big targets. But the tracker Marines were very proud of their vehicles. There was a strange relationship between the infantry "grunts" and the trackers. Most trackers believed that their vehicles were their domain and that it was the vehicle commander's job to "captain" the track. They believed that while they were moving, they were in charge and the infantry Marines were only passengers in "their" vehicle. In fact, the trackers had their own independent command structure. Each vehicle had a commander. Each three tracks had a section leader, which was usually the most senior of the track commanders in that section. One of the track commanders was the AAV platoon sergeant and another was the platoon leader. While moving, either on land or in the water, the AAV platoon maneuvered and fought as an armored platoon.

Once they arrived at their destination, the infantry commanders would deploy their troops and the trackers would provide covering fire to the grunts on the ground. One of LtCol. Rickey Grabowski's greatest challenges during CAX would be to integrate his infantry Marines and tracker Marines into a single fighting force that could quickly switch from AAV to infantry command and back again.

Another challenge would be to integrate tanks into his fighting force. The M1A1 Abrams tank is 70 tons and provides unequaled armor protection. Propelled by a helicopter turbine engine, it carries a 155mm gun controlled by a fire control system that can point and shoot on the run at a moving target over 1.6km (1 mile) away, and hit with the first shot – every time. If the main gun isn't fierce enough, the crew also has a .50 cal. and 240G 7.62mm machine gun aboard.

The battalion staff had several choices as to how they would use their tanks within the battalion. The tank company could be kept together and used as a fourth maneuver unit. It could be broken up and a platoon given to each infantry company, or Grabowski could use a combination of the two formations. He decided to use a concept employed by the Army and developed company teams. Two of his three companies would remain pure mechanized infantry, each company riding in 12 AAVs. Bravo Company would be split up and mixed with his tank company to produce two independent teams. Team Tank would be tank heavy, containing two tank platoons and the two additional command tanks (ten tanks in all) married with a single infantry platoon, riding in three AMTRACs. Team Mech would consist of the remaining Bravo Company infantry platoons and its weapons platoon, and infantry company command, all riding in nine tracks plus a single tank platoon of four M1A1 tanks.

This gave the Timberwolves four major maneuver units: Alpha Company, Charlie Company, Team Tank, and Team Mech. Grabowski also had a weapons company to integrate into his mechanized infantry battalion. The weapons company contained snipers, assault teams with heavy machine guns, and SMAW rockets, Javelin missile teams, the battalion's 81mm mortar platoon and the battalion's only armored HMMWVs (High Mobility Multi-Wheeled Vehicle, or "Hummer.") The 16 armored HMMWVs were split into two eight-vehicle Combined Anti-Armor Teams (CAAT).

Each CAAT had four vehicle-mounted TOW missile launchers and four scout vehicles with either .50 cal. machine guns or MK-19 grenade launchers. All the CAAT vehicles carried an additional SAW. Grabowski's CAAT sections were the most versatile in the entire battalion. The fast and agile HMMWVs could be used as scout vehicles or as a fast-moving anti-armor force. The teams of eight could be broken down into sections of four vehicles or pairs of two to provide wide-ranging protection for the battalion's flanks. They could be quickly repositioned to deal with new threats or conditions on the battlefield. CAAT was Grabowski's most nimble maneuver unit.

The battalion's organic artillery asset was its 81mm mortar platoon. Eight HMMWVs each carried an 81mm mortar team. Wherever Grabowski

ABOVE **A small electric turret, or "up-gun" perched above a Marine AMTRAC houses a .50 cal. machine gun and a MK19 automatic grenade launcher. The track commander typically mans the up-gun. (Photo courtesy USMC)**

went on the battlefield, the "81s" were sure to be close by. Grabowski spread the remaining assets of his weapons company throughout his infantry companies. The sniper teams, 240G machine gun teams, and assault teams with their SMAW and Javelin rockets were spread evenly among Alpha, Bravo, and Charlie companies, giving his company commanders even more firepower and flexibility.

CAX was the perfect environment to work out all of these details and to pull everyone together into a fighting battalion. The exercises started small, with infantrymen at company level working with trackers and tankers on the little details that would make the difference in a real fight. The trackers and infantrymen practiced loading up, movement, stopping in a herringbone formation, and deploying Marines. They practiced what to do if an AMTRAC were to break down. Their "jump track" drills were like a rehearsed "Chinese fire drill" (a dangerous stunt of disembarking from a vehicle while stopped at a traffic light, a popular term and trick in the US during the 1960s). Every Marine knew where to go, as they would leave a small team with the broken-down vehicle, grab essential equipment and split the remaining Marines between the other two tracks in the platoon. The two remaining tracks would be crowded, but no one would be left behind.

As the exercises progressed, the company commanders practiced employing other weapons through their Fire Support Team (FiST). The FiST travels with the company commander in his command track, some ride in the company's mortar track. Each infantry company has its own organic 60mm light mortars. They are the company commanders' personal indirect fire asset and can quickly supply supporting fire, smoke, and illumination to the infantry. It is the job of the FiST to coordinate any heavier support from other units.

The FiST leader is the company's weapons platoon leader. He has radiomen and Marines to assist him in maintaining situational awareness and communications with his company commander, the battalion 81mm mortar platoon, supporting artillery units, and aircraft providing close-air-support. The FiST usually has two other officers, a Forward Observer (FO) and a Forward Air Controller (FAC). The FO is attached if there is a Marine artillery unit taking part in the operation and two of the three infantry companies have a FAC attached.

The FO is an officer on loan to the infantry company from the supporting artillery unit. He knows all of the officers in the artillery unit and can provide an artilleryman's perspective on the battle back to his unit. Likewise, all FACs are Marine aviators who rotate to an infantry unit for a tour of duty. The FAC program is one of the most important factors contributing to the Corps' ability to provide over-the-shoulder close air support. The FACs on the ground learn what it is like to be on the receiving end of close air support, and they "talk the talk" of the pilots in the air. This close communication between air and ground units produces an air-ground combat force unequaled in the world.

Once the Marines on the ground were comfortable working with one another, the companies moved on to real combined arms exercises. The FiSTs trained long hours on planning missions and ensuring smooth cooperation between the aircraft and artillery. Here is where the United States Marine Corps excels. It takes true professionals to fight in a combined arms environment. The weapons that can be employed on a single call for fire are lethal: a misplaced air-to-ground missile or artillery barrage could be deadly to the Marines on the ground. Remember, "friendly fire" is anything but. A CAX is the only place that FOs, FACs, air

BELOW **A Sea Stallion helicopter training in the Southern California desert during a Combined Arms Exercise. (Photo courtesy USMC)**

officers, Fire Support Coordinators (FSCs), and company and battalion commanders can hone their combined arms skills. So, much of the time at CAX is devoted to integrating artillery and aircraft into the MAGTF.

After many days of training, the entire battalion came together for a final exercise (FINEX). Here the battalion's staff would try to bring it all together. The battalion Air Officer (AO) would orchestrate the air battle, handing over incoming aircraft to his FACs. The FSC would choreograph the indirect fire battle, using his company FOs and the battalion's 81mm mortars. The FSC and AO needed to maintain constant communication to coordinate the two battles. Without synchronization, a flying artillery shell could hit an incoming helicopter. All the while, the battalion commander and his staff needed to maintain situational awareness of the air, ground, and artillery battle, and direct their maneuver units toward winning their objectives. Even in training, directing a Marine infantry battalion was not an easy task. It took the concerted, coordinated effort of dozens of professional Marine officers and the cool head and lightning-fast decision-making skills of its battalion commander.

The Timberwolves passed their final exercise with flying colors. Christmas was rapidly approaching when Duncan, Johnson, and the Timberwolves returned to Camp Lejeune. Johnson and Duncan planned to fly home to Atlanta together. Duncan and Johnson were both promoted to corporal in December 2002. It was no surprise to anyone in the company. Capt. Wittnam personally pinned on their new rank in a small ceremony at a company muster one morning. Then, he made the announcement. "It looks like there is a possibility that the President could order us to Iraq." The company reacted with enthusiasm. Wittnam went on, "The battalion commander has told me that anyone who has leave should take the holiday time to be with family. Everyone must be back by January 6. Dismissed." Charlie Company scattered. Marines got on their cell phones or rushed to public phones to make their holiday arrangements.

DEPLOYMENT

Onslow Beach, North Carolina

After a decade of budget cutbacks, the 2d Marine Regiment was short of equipment and personnel. They would have a hard time putting a complete RCT together at this short notice. The 2d Battalion had already deployed with an MEU, leaving the regiment with only two infantry battalions, and 3d Battalion's "Betio Bastards," who were short by nearly 100 Marines. The commanding general of the 2d Marine Expeditionary Brigade scrambled to fill the 2d Marines' ranks. He reached across Camp Lejeune and "chopped" the 2d Battalion of the Eighth Marine Regiment ("America's Battalion") to the 2d Marines. Then he contacted Camp Geiger at New River and graduated scores of young Marines from the SOI several weeks early.

By the time Duncan and Johnson returned from their holiday break, the Marines of the regiment were mobilizing. There were several days of mayhem, working from before dawn to well after the sun went down, preparing to embark the entire regiment. Paperwork needed to be filled out. Beneficiaries were updated on insurance policies. Wills had to be

completed and signed. Equipment needed to be inventoried, inspected, and packed, and Marines had to be loaded aboard their ships.

The 2d Tank Battalion, all but one company of the 2d Light Armored Reconnaissance Battalion, and the 2d AAV Battalion, had already been reallocated to the 1st Marine Division. The regiment would have to make do with a single LAR and AAV Company. With no tank units left at Camp Lejeune, the general asked for Marine reserve units to fill in. Alpha Company of the 8th Marine Reserve Tank Battalion was called to report for duty. Within 72 hours, they had assembled at Fort Knox and were bussed to North Carolina just in time to embark on their ships.

The US Navy swung into action in the first week of 2003 and sent seven ships of Amphibious Task Force-East (ATF-E) to the waters off the North Carolina coast. Three of the seven were "big deck" ships: USS *Bataan*, USS *Saipan*, and USS *Kearsarge* were some of the largest craft in the US Navy. They looked like aircraft carriers, but were actually specially designed to carry Marine aircraft – helicopters and Vertical Take Off and Landing (VTOL) Harriers. In addition to their massive flight deck and aircraft hangar decks, these ships had a "well deck." The entire aft end of the ship could be flooded down and giant stern doors could be opened to allow Marine amphibious vehicles and landing craft to swim in and out of the ship.

While USS *Portland*, USS *Ashland*, USS *Ponce*, and USS *Gunston Hall* did not have flight decks, they did have well decks and small helicopter landing pads. The fleet, which became known as the "Magnificent Seven," loaded over 7,000 battle-ready Marines of the 2d MEB. They turned eastward and headed out on a month-long journey that would take Task Force Tarawa half way around the world to fight a modern-day war along the ancient banks of the Euphrates River.

Even with the reserve tank company, the regiment only had enough vehicles to "mech-up" a single battalion. The Timberwolves were selected to lead the regiment, so they were given the armor assets. The reserve tankers of Alpha Company, 8th Tanks and their 14 M1A1 tanks were assigned to the 1st Battalion. Alpha Company of the 2d Assault Amphibian Battalion was also chopped to 1/2 with its 40 AMTRACs, enough to transport all three of the 1st Battalion's infantry companies. Col. Ron Bailey's other two infantry battalions would have to ride in 7-ton trucks.

Duncan and Johnson ended up on the oldest of the ships of the "Magnificent Seven", the USS *Ponce*. It was a miserable trip. The Marines were packed into berthing areas from the deck to the overhead. There was no way to get any privacy. They had to wait in line for chow, to take a shower, to mail a letter, or to use the few telephones available for calling home. They continued to train in the ship's well deck. The highlight of the day would be when they were ordered topside for PT or a ship's drill. Most of their days were spent below decks in the crowded troop areas. At least the Navy food was good.

The Marines longed to arrive at their destination and to get off the crowded ship. They passed the time by working out, playing video and board games, and watching war movies. Duncan and Johnson spent long hours talking about the coming war. Each day brought a host of new rumors – Saddam had been killed or he had fled the country – but the serious conversation centered on the debate in the United Nations. Would the international body avoid war? The Marines wondered out loud whether they would be committed to battle or sent back the way they came. They also talked about going into battle. Duncan and Johnson had been training for over a year for the coming battle – others much longer. They all wondered how they would react to the sound of hostile fire.

They worried whether they would live up to the traditions of the Marine Corps or if they would falter, or, worse yet, cower. They were Marines. They all knew that they could not let the Corps down: *Honor, Courage, Commitment*. They all prayed they would live up to their core values. As the days rolled past, the flotilla negotiated the Straits of Gibraltar and then the Suez Canal.

Security was tight through these narrow passages. Sniper and machine gun teams lined the rails of the ships. Once through the canal, the uniform of the day changed to desert camouflage. The mood of the Marines and crew changed too. The Marines became more serious as it became clearer that they were actually going to war. The ships' crewmembers began treating the Marines with more respect, and the everyday bantering between the sailors and Marines all but stopped.

In the desert

Finally, ATF-E arrived at its destination, the Kuwaiti Naval Base just south of Kuwait City. The 2d MEB quickly unloaded and headed for the camps located in the northern Kuwaiti desert. As 2d MEB arrived, they found that all of their air assets had been reallocated to the 3d Marine Air Wing to support the overall I MEF effort in the invasion. 2d MEB was renamed Task Force Tarawa. With the loss of Marine Air Group-29 and most of its service support battalion, Task Force Tarawa was little more than a partially reinforced Marine infantry regiment.

Charlie Company drove through Kuwait for hours, avoiding the populated areas. It was nearly nightfall when Duncan, Johnson and the rest of Charlie Company arrived at Camp Shoup, which was little more than a spit of sand in the middle of the desert. The Seabees (naval

ABOVE **Marines training on flight deck of USS *Saipan* while in transit from their North Carolina home to war in Iraq. The M16A2 rifle was the most commonly used weapon by the Marines in *Iraqi Freedom*. It has many advantages: it is lightweight and air-cooled, with an accurate firing range of 500 meters. It also has many disadvantages. It does not pack a very heavy punch. Several rounds are required to stop a charging enemy soldier. It is also prone to jamming in the sandy desert. (Photo courtesy Capt. Eric Griggs USMC)**

construction battalion) had scraped up a berm all around the perimeter and a dozen General Purpose (GP) tents dotted the inside of the camp. Dozens more were being erected as Duncan and Johnson rolled to a stop.

"This is it." The first sergeant announced. 1st Sgt. Jose Henao was a native of South America. He had moved to the US with his parents when he was a teenager. He loved his adopted country, knowing what it was like to grow up in a lawless land. At 18, there was no question in his mind. He joined the Marine Corps, hoping that one day he could return and bring peace to his native land. Now, nearly 20 years later, he was the senior enlisted man in Charlie Company.

Every man in the 1st Battalion devoted the next several days to setting up camp. They erected massive GP tents with Marine Corps' precision in straight rows. There were no floors in the tents, no air conditioning, and the Marines lived out of their sleeping bags on the sandy floor. Some enterprising men found discarded sheets of plywood, which they strategically placed like bedroom throw rugs.

They built a chow hall tent and set up latrines. Once they had settled in, they began daily schedules filled with training, sending out security patrols, manning Camp Shoup's security posts and PT. LtCol. Grabowski wanted to keep his men busy – it would help pass the time. In their leisure time, the men fashioned baseballs out of tape and played stickball. They had organized boxing and wrestling matches and movies.

One enterprising tank platoon leader found a Pizza Hut at a larger camp farther to the rear. He and his wingman bought a dozen pizzas and a case of Pepsi and brought it back to their Marines. That night, Blue Platoon had a party of sorts. The entire platoon gathered in the Blue's tent and ate cold pizza, drank warm Pepsis, and chatted long into the night through one of the worst sandstorms of their stay. Sandstorms occurred regularly, and some were worse than others. At best, they

would embed a fine powder in everything. At worst, they would rip tent stakes from the ground and blow down tents.

It didn't take long for the Marines of Task Force Tarawa to start talking of how good they had it on the ships. Living in the Kuwaiti desert waiting to go to war was a miserable experience. Then the mail arrived and morale improved immediately. Soon embedded reporters arrived who would be traveling to war with the Marines. They had advanced equipment that would allow them to transmit live from the battlefield. They also had satellite telephones, which they often let the Marines use to call home.

ABOVE **American military encampment in the northern Kuwaiti desert. This was just one of many camps that were sprinkled throughout northern Kuwait. The camps were often hit by sandstorms, making the lives of the Marines very uncomfortable. (Photo courtesy Capt. Eric Griggs USMC)**

LEFT **RCT-2 Marines cleaning their weapons in Camp Shoup in preparation for their attack into Iraq. (Courtesy of Joe Muccia USMC)**

On the morning of March 19, there was a flurry of activity around the camp. The entire regiment was packing up to move. Vehicles were being loaded and some of the tents broken down. Task Force Tarawa's orders had come in. On the 20th, RCT-2 would move to Assembly Area Hawkins at the Kuwaiti border. On the morning of the 21st, they would attack into Iraq.

INTO BATTLE

On March 21, 2003, V Corps swept northwest through the Iraqi desert to a last-minute turn toward Baghdad through the Karbala Gap, while the Marines of I MEF would cross the Euphrates at An Nasiriyah. They would charge up the Tigris River along the classic invasion route that the British used in World War I. The first battle of An Nasiriyah during World War I was a bloody fight between the British and the Turks. The British captured the city, losing 500 dead and killing as many Turks, as well as an untold number of Nasiriyans. Now, history would repeat itself, as the 2d Marine Regiment charged out of the Arabian desert toward this ancient city. Task Force Tarawa would "kick open the door" and the entire 1st Marine Division would cross the Euphrates and race toward the center of Saddam Hussein's power – Baghdad.

An Nasiriyah was the first Iraqi population center on the road from Kuwait to Baghdad. Its population was primarily Shi'ite Muslims who were not sympathetic to Saddam Hussein and his regime. American war planners hoped that the Iraqis in An Nasiriyah would surrender with little or no resistance.

While hoping for a quick success, the 2d Marine Regiment's commanders planned for a fight for control of the bridges across the Euphrates River. 1st Battalion had been reinforced with tanks and AMTRACs, and the Timberwolves had planned to seize the eastern bridges regardless of the amount of resistance.

Task Force Tarawa Marine

Recruit Training

Camp Shoup

E

Med-evac

F

After two long days of traveling across the Iraqi desert in the cramped confines of their hated AMTRAC, Duncan and Johnson were about as miserable as they had ever been. They would rather be back in the Crucible at Parris Island than riding in this hot metal deathtrap. Late on March 22, they had stopped for the night in an open area at the edge of the desert. Small tufts of grass sprinkled the landscape – a sign that water was nearby. They stopped well after sunset, deployed Marines for security, and dug in for the night. Duncan and his squad dug another fighting position out of the soft, gravelly sand, and set a watch while the others tried to get some sleep. Johnson drifted off to sleep for what seemed like only a few minutes when the first sergeant woke him. "Mount up," he told Johnson, and then moved on to another squad. Johnson woke the

remaining members of his squad, and they packed up and climbed into C211 with their gear. Rumor had it that today's trip would be short.

As the night of the 22nd became the morning of the 23rd, the battalion was ahead of schedule. Everyone could see a string of lights on a nearby highway. The Army was moving west with their headlights on as though they were on a weekend maneuver up I-95 in the middle of a rush hour. Capt. Wittnam had told Duncan that they only had to move about 40km (24.8 miles) to their blocking position just south of a town along the Euphrates River.

Johnson and Duncan were both assigned to the 3d Platoon of Capt. Wittnam's Charlie Company, but since their promotions to corporal, they were separated when they both became assistant squad leaders. It is always very strange for a Marine not to have his buddy at his shoulder, but their new ranks brought new responsibilities, and each worked hard at becoming a good NCO.

Capt. Wittnam had 12 tracks to carry his company, C201–C212. Each squad of the first platoon rode in C201, C202, and C203. Second platoon's squads were assigned to C205, C206, and C207. Lt. Mike Seely's 3d Platoon manned C209, C210, and C211. Johnson and his squad rode in C211, while Duncan's squad had been assigned to C209. Lt. Seely was a hard-charging Marine. His men worshiped him. They often commented that they would follow Lt. Seely and Capt. Wittnam into hell.

Third Platoon was Capt. Wittnam's "go-to" platoon, so he planned for C209, C210, and C211 to take the lead of the company when they entered An Nasiriyah. Wittnam would follow 3d Platoon in his company command track, C204. The weapons platoon leader would follow Wittnam with the company FiST team and a portion of the mortar section in the mortar track, C208. They would be followed by 1st and 2d platoons while the company first sergeant would take up the rear of the column with the ambulance track, C212, and a couple of HMMWVs.

As Charlie Company mounted up, the night was black and clear. Billions of pinheads of light punctured the blackened night sky. As they waited in the Iraqi desert, Capt. Wittnam went through the plan in his head for the thousandth time.

An Nasiriyah

The 2d Marine Regiment and its battalion staffs had been planning this mission since they were at sea. Everyone anticipated little resistance in An Nasiriyah, but still planned for the worst. RCT-2 would approach An Nasiriyah from the south. The 1st Battalion would move to within 16km (10 miles) of the Eastern Euphrates River Bridge and establish a defensive line. At the same time, 3d Battalion would drive northwest along Iraq's Highway 1 and relieve 3d Infantry Division Units who had taken the Highway 1 bridge over the Euphrates River the day before. With 3d Battalion holding the Highway 1 bridge 16km (10 miles) west of An Nasiriyah, 2d Marines would wait for the order to move north to secure the eastern bridges through the city.

On command, 2d Battalion, 8th Marines would move up behind the Timberwolves as they raced to secure the Euphrates River and Saddam Canal Bridge. During the planning stage, the primary concern centered on the 4km (2.5 miles) urban stretch between the Euphrates River and the Saddam Canal, which bordered the city on the north. Early on in the planning, it was dubbed "the Mogadishu Mile" and then "Ambush Alley."

ABOVE **Charlie Company Marines dug in to muddy fighting holes after a rainy night north of An Nasiriyah. (Photo courtesy of Joe Raedle/Getty Images)**

The 4km (2.5 miles) stretch was lined with buildings set back on both sides of the road. Scores of alleyways and hundreds of windows and doorways provided ample cover for Iraqi fighters. So, the Marines decided that if they encountered resistance, they would take a hard right turn after they crossed the Euphrates and they would skirt the built-up areas in An Nasiriyah on the east side of town.

Alpha Company would cross the bridge first and move into positions to defend the Euphrates River Bridge. Team Tank would follow Alpha over the first bridge, followed by Team Mech. The battalion commander would follow the lead companies in his HMMWV, two command tracks, and a dozen other small trucks. Charlie Company would be the last across the Euphrates.

Capt. Wittnam had two alternate courses of action. The first was to follow the battalion command and the lead companies off to the east, or, if resistance was light, follow the lead companies straight through Ambush Alley. Charlie Company's mission was to secure the Saddam Canal Bridge in the north. Either way, all Wittnam had to do was follow

Grabowski's command group over the Euphrates River and continue on track until they reached the Saddam Canal.

By 3am on March 23, 2003, the Timberwolves were moving. They drove up onto a paved road and headed north. They passed a large intersection with Highway 1 and continued north. LtCol. Grabowski halted his armored column just north of a cloverleaf intersection and waited for a report from his operations officer that all of the battalion's vehicles had made it north of the intersection.

Standing on the darkened road, LtCol. Grabowski looked south and could not believe the sight before him. A column of trucks was racing north with headlights blazing. Marines are not supposed to travel in war zones with their headlights on; in fact, they are not supposed to show any lights. Grabowski was at first furious. Then he learned that these were not vehicles from his battalion.

His orders were to relieve a unit of the 3d Infantry Division which was to have preceded him up Route Moe (Highway 7) the day before, so he reasoned that these were 3d Infantry Division vehicles. Grabowski ordered the road cleared as 18 Army vehicles raced by like they were late for payday.

Several soldiers in the vehicles wondered as they passed why they were overtaking combat units. This was the doomed 507th Maintenance Company. Their company commander was hopelessly lost. He should have taken his column northwest on Highway 1 at the intersection. Instead, he followed, then passed, Grabowski's Marines. As the 507th disappeared in the Iraqi darkness, the Timberwolves moved up on the road and headed north to their first objective, the 20th Northing.

The US military has segmented maps of the entire earth into 100km grid squares. Each 100km square has a unique designation. The city of An Nasiriyah is located in the 38RPV grid square. More precisely, the eastern Euphrates River Bridge is located at 38RPV 209 344. When using a three-number grid coordinate system, each increment signifies 100 meters and the grids are read from west to east and south to north. 38RPV 000 000 would lie at the southwest corner of the grid square, and 38RPV 999 999 would lie at the northeast corner.

RIGHT **LtCol. Rickey Grabowski talks with the Timberwolves at Camp Shoup on the day before they move north to invade Iraq.** (Photo courtesy of Joe Raedle/Getty Images)

So the coordinate in our example would read 38RPV, a unique quadrant on the face of the earth, 209 East and 344 North. Airmen, soldiers, sailors and Marines break down the coordinates into 1km gridlines. The bridge in An Nasiriyah is approximately at the 21st Easting and almost halfway between the 34th and 35th Northing.

The Timberwolves arrived at the 20th Northing an hour ahead of schedule and began to organize their defenses. Alpha and Charlie Companies fanned out on either side of the road. The ground was muddy and several tracks became stuck. They were pulled out and moved to drier ground.

The countryside was so wet that 1st Battalion, 10th Marines artillery had no place to set up behind the Timberwolves, so LtCol. Grabowski requested permission to push forward another 2km (1.2 miles) to the 22nd Northing, to make room for the big 155mm guns.

As Team Tank moved out, they came under fire. The Iraqis had positioned their southernmost scouts in mud-brick buildings on either side of the road leading into town. Machine gun and small-arms fire erupted around Grabowski's lead tanks and CAAT vehicles.

Meanwhile, the 507th had traveled over the eastern Euphrates River Bridge, all the way north through Ambush Alley, over the Saddam Canal Bridge, continuing north another 1km (0.6 miles) to Highway 16. They turned left and drove another 2.5km (1.5 miles) before they encountered another "T" intersection. They turned right and went a short distance north before the 507th's commander finally realized he was lost.

He commanded his soldiers to lock-and-load and to turn the convoy around. By now, every Iraqi with a gun in the entire city was awake. The 507th's return journey would be very different. As they made their first left turn to retrace their path, the Iraqis opened fire from both sides of the road. Iraqi army regulars and black-clad armed men were everywhere.

BELOW **A Marine speaks through an interpreter with local Iraqi camel herders just south of An Nasiriyah on March 23, 2003. The Marines are taught to use many skills beyond fieldcraft and fighting, one of the primary of these being negotiation and diplomacy. (Courtesy of Kevin Ellicot USMC)**

They were running up on the road, some trying to get in front of the vehicles, others trying to grab on and climb aboard. The doomed convoy accelerated, trying to get out of the "kill zone."

The enemy raced behind the convoy in pickup trucks. In the lead, the company commander's HMMWV missed the turn south that would take them back to the Saddam Canal Bridge. As the lead vehicles continued east, others realized that the commander had missed his turn. They radioed ahead to alert him and then the convoy had to turn around again.

The company commander turned his agile HMMWV quickly, as did the next two lead vehicles. As they raced back west, they passed the other doomed trucks. As they approached the turn south, the Iraqis were driving headlong into the Americans. The Americans turned hard left, just as the Iraqi pickups veered right. The second US 5-ton truck sideswiped the Iraqi technical, knocking it off the road. Then the three US trucks raced south, over the Saddam Canal, through Ambush Alley, and back over the Euphrates River Bridge, all the while dodging obstacles and Iraqi soldiers and taking heavy fire.

They raced south for another 2km (1.2 miles) and over a railroad bridge, which was being defended by a company of Iraqi tanks and infantry. All three vehicles were now bullet-ridden and some had blazing tires. One of the soldiers noticed a US tank in the distance and nervously thought to himself, "Man, I hope he doesn't shoot, 'cause M1 tanks don't miss."

Team Tank had nearly silenced the enemy fire when one of the tank gunners saw trucks approaching from the north. He trained his main gun, ready to fire, and then he realized that they were US vehicles. Team Tank held its fire and Capt. Troy King and the three lead vehicles raced south and skidded to a stop at the Marines' position.

"We were ambushed," he told Maj. Bill Peeples, the Marine tank commander. "I have soldiers still up there," he exclaimed, as he motioned north, back up the road. Maj. Peeples remounted his tank and ordered his tank platoon forward. Under increasing fire, they raced up the road to find several abandoned vehicles just south of a railroad bridge.

BELOW **1/2 Marines wait alongside the road for orders to move into An Nasiriyah on March 23, 2003. (Courtesy of Kevin Ellicot USMC)**

They found ten soldiers hunkered down in a trench along the side of the road. Maj. Peeples pulled his tank up next to the soldiers and another of his tanks flanked the soldiers on the other side of their trench. Marines jumped from their tanks to help the beleaguered soldiers. Alpha Company sent their ambulance track forward to evacuate the wounded. All the while, the tankers were locked in a gun battle with the Iraqi defenders.

Team Tank's FAC reported "Marines in Contact," and Cobra helicopters swarmed into the battle. "Hawk" directed the Marine pilots toward enemy vehicles in the western tree line and requested that they search along the road for more stranded soldiers. The attack helicopters and tanks proved too much for the defenders and the Iraqi survivors quickly faded away into the desert.

LtCol. Grabowski ordered his tanks back to refuel and his infantry companies to clear the buildings on either side of the road. Then he began to set his battalion into defensive positions so that he could hold this position until he received the order to move north and secure the bridges in An Nasiriyah. No sooner had the tanks headed south than the regimental and brigade commanders showed up at Grabowski's CP.

When told of the ambush, BGen. Richard Natonski ordered the Timberwolves forward. Grabowski ordered his Team Mech, minus their platoon of tanks, and one of his CAAT teams forward. Bravo Company pushed ahead with a cordon of CAAT vehicles. They reached the railroad bridge and, as the first track crested the bridge, the battalion radio net crackled, "TANKS! We have enemy tanks on both sides of the road." The column halted, the lead track backed down from the crest of the bridge and several CAAT HMMWVs raced up onto the bridge. They opened fire with their .50 cal. machine guns while the TOW gunners zeroed in with their deadly missiles and fired. The missiles screamed across the battlefield, trailing a wake of smoke. A direct hit, one tank down. The TOW vehicles worked in a round-robin fashion. After firing, the HMMWV would drive down off the bridge to be replaced with a ready TOW vehicle. The Marines were reloading, zeroing in, and firing in rapid succession.

Soon, nine Iraqi tanks lay silent on the battlefield. Tanks were not the only threat at the bridge. Iraqi machine gunners were firing on the Marines from buildings on either side of the road. Black-clad figures

BELOW **1/2 Marines deploy south of An Nasiriyah on March 23, 2003. Cobra helicopters are waiting for their turn to support the Marines further north. (Photo courtesy Capt. Harold Qualkinbush USMC)**

could be seen lobbing mortar shells at the Marines from a distant roof, and small-arms fire was coming from many locations. Bravo Company and the CAAT teams poured continuous streams of fire downrange toward the enemy. More Cobras and fixed-wing aircraft swooped into the battle, directed by Bravo Company's FAC – "Mouth."

The Marines defeated a dug in tank company that was supported by infantry and heavy weapons in short order. Within half an hour, the fighting had subsided to intermittent sniper fire. Grabowski had Alpha and Charlie Companies fan out again during the fight. Bravo Company and CAAT held the road, and Alpha and Charlie tracks protected the flanks. LtCol. Grabowski was not going any further until his tanks returned to lead the way. The Timberwolves waited for what seemed like an eternity until the first platoon of tanks appeared. Team Tank and CAAT immediately pushed over the Railroad Bridge toward Nasiriyah. Bravo Company's Team Mech followed Team Tank. Grabowski's Alpha Command Group fell in behind Team Mech. Alpha Company moved back up onto the raised highway behind Grabowski. Charlie Company ended up last in the armored column. This would change the planned order of assault on the Euphrates River Bridge. Bravo Company and the Command Group would be first across the river, followed by Alpha Company. Charlie Company would have to keep in touch with their battalion commander to know which route they had taken.

As Charlie Company was moving up onto the road, C209 aborted. It just quit moving. Third Squad had trained for this in CAX and in Kuwait. They quickly abandoned the dead track, leaving a fire team to protect the crippled vehicle, and jumped aboard C210 and C211. When Charlie Company's lead platoon was forced to stop, Capt. Wittnam ordered 1st Platoon into the lead. The 1st and 2d platoons rolled past Seely, Duncan, Johnson, and the rest of 3d Platoon as they scrambled to board C210 and C211.

Seely took over as the infantry commander in C211, while Duncan jumped into the back of Johnson's track. The troop compartment was well over capacity and Marines climbed onto the roof of the track to make room for the extra men. Duncan and Johnson climbed over Marines and forced their way forward and up onto the bench. They were standing between the legs of the Marines sitting inside, unable to move their feet without pushing the Marines below aside.

Duncan and Johnson stood back to back at the front of the track, M16s resting on the sandbags that were used for additional protection. Duncan was right behind Seely. He could hear him yelling at his driver, "Push! Push! Push!" C211 lurched forward and raced north trying to catch the tail end of the company.

Across the Euphrates

CAAT and Team Tank reached the Euphrates River first. They drove up on the large structure to find the city of An Nasiriyah and Ambush Alley ahead. From his position several vehicles back, Grabowski thought, "There is no turning back now. We are committed." As soon as the CAAT HMMWVs and the tanks reached the northern bank of the Euphrates, all hell broke loose. Flashes erupted from every window and doorway. More enemy fire rained down from sandbagged rooftop positions, and shots rang out from the southern bank of the river.

The Marines opened fire with everything they had and immediately took a hard right turn toward the eastern side of the city. Vehicles continued to pour over the Euphrates River Bridge behind Team Tank. Bravo Company's remaining tracks clanged over the bridge. Then LtCol. Grabowski was up on the bridge racing forward into a fierce battle. The two command tracks drove into the city, followed by the dozen HMMWVs in the colonel's entourage. They all took a right turn and disappeared into the narrow alleyways on the eastern side of the highway.

The alleys were so narrow that the tanks were knocking over carts, and at the narrowest points crumbling walls just to get through. As Bravo Company and the command group pushed to the east, Alpha Company crested the bridge. When they reached the northern bank, they fanned out on either side of the road and stopped. Bullets continued to fly.

A212 was the last track over. Inside the trailing track, Alpha Company's first sergeant noticed a civilian taxi following them over the bridge. He and several other Marines frantically waved to the taxi driver to go back. They didn't want civilians to venture into the firefight. As they motioned, the taxi crested the bridge and four Iraqis jumped out and began firing at them. The Marines returned fire, killing all four. Seconds later another taxi appeared. It was immediately taken out. The Timberwolves had captured the Euphrates River Bridge, but now they were surrounded.

The Marines in Alpha Company's tracks nervously waited in the hot metal boxes. Finally, the familiar order came, "Dismount!" and each track's heavy metal ramp fell. The Marines poured out as the entire rifle company deployed. As Alpha Company's Marines fought to defend their newly captured prizes; Bravo Company reached the eastern edge of the city and open terrain. They fanned out into an open field. The tracks groaned and slowed, then stopped. They were stuck. Some had sunk in muck to their chassis. There was no time to warn the others – tanks sunk to a halt, and HMMWVs slid into the gooey mess. The eastern thrust was

LEFT **2d Battalion, 8th Division Marines on the Southeastern Euphrates River Bridge on the morning of March 24, 2003. Note that they are dressed in full woodland camouflage MOPP gear, with webbing, and the Marine on the far left is carrying his M16A2 rifle. (Photo courtesy USMC)**

completely bogged down. Many vehicles sat motionless. Then the eastern rooftops erupted with sniper fire.

More and more buildings popped up along the road as Charlie Company reached the suburban outskirts of An Nasiriyah. They passed an industrialized area with warehouses on the left and large oil storage tanks on the right. As they were approaching a lush stand of date palms, they noticed the largest structure they had seen since leaving Kuwait. Just as they closed on the rear of Alpha Company, they saw a large concrete bridge rising in the distance: the Euphrates River Bridge had to be at least four stories tall.

C2110 and C211 ground forward, now at the tail end of the company and the battalion. Duncan could see Charlie's lead track crest the bridge. Just as C201 disappeared from sight, shots rang out. At first the reports were in the distance. The Iraqis must have been firing from north of the Euphrates. Then to Duncan's surprise, he heard cracks. The sound was identical to the mini sonic booms in the butts. Then he heard the ping of metal hitting metal. C211 was being shot at. Every minute or so, another ping or crack would get Duncan's attention.

LtCol. Grabowski tried to radio Charlie Company to warn Capt. Wittnam not to come east, but he could not get through on the radio. He tried and tried to contact Wittnam, but there was no answer. Capt. Wittnam was pressing over the Euphrates River Bridge behind Alpha Company. As Wittnam crested the bridge, he could see Alpha Company in defensive positions below, but Bravo Company was nowhere in sight.

Wittnam made a command decision in the blink of an eye. He ordered Charlie Company straight up Ambush Alley. After all, his orders were to secure the Saddam Canal Bridge, and he thought that Bravo Company had probably gone straight north. Even if they hadn't, his commander's intent was clear. Charlie was to secure the northern bridge.

BELOW **3d Battalion, 2d Division Marines moving through the breach in the border berm between Kuwait and Iraq. (Photo courtesy Capt. Harold Qualkinbush USMC)**

Casualties

Charlie Company pushed straight ahead through Ambush Alley, C201 encountering the fiercest fire. Almost every new alleyway sheltered an RPG or machine-gun team. Rocket trails filled the street. Some whizzed wildly into the sky, others were near misses. A few RPGs hit their target with a thud and did not explode. The gunner in the lead track was firing at everything and anything in his path.

Armed Iraqis poured into the streets, wildly firing AK-47s, RPGs, and machine guns at the advancing armored column. The Marines were returning the fire with even greater ferocity and deadly accuracy. All the while, Charlie Company's tracks kept moving. An amazing 11 of the 12 tracks made it through the gauntlet. Duncan and Johnson could see the Saddam Canal Bridge in the distance when a thunderous explosion rocked the vehicle. An enemy RPG had finally found its mark. The rocket hit in the right rear of the track and spewed hot shrapnel into the crowded troop compartment. All Johnson could see was smoke billowing out of the troop compartment. "Glass is dead," one Marine yelled out.

Lt. Seely slapped the track driver on his helmet. "Go! Go! Go," he ordered. Then he asked Duncan how many casualties there were, but Duncan couldn't tell. There was too much smoke pouring out of the track. He only knew that the Marine next to him had been hit. He was screaming in pain. Duncan and Johnson both lifted the wounded Marine up onto the track roof. His right leg was bleeding heavily; a large metal shard had sliced into his thigh. Johnson quickly tied a tourniquet around his leg to slow the bleeding.

Meanwhile, Sgt. Bitz, C211's driver, was racing forward at full speed. He was driving over, around and through obstacles in his path. He passed a couple of tracks and drove up over the Saddam Canal Bridge, trailing a column of oily black smoke. He raced over the bridge and ground the crippled vehicle to a halt right in the middle of the road, about 200 meters north of the canal.

Seely hit Bitz on the helmet again, "Drop the ramp. Drop the ramp." The grenade had damaged the ramp and it would not open. Seely jumped from his hatch and moved along the top of the troop compartment. "Get out! Get out," he ordered.

Sgt. William Schafer had been riding in C201 at the head of the Company. C211 had come to rest within meters of Schafer's track. He ran over and opened the small back door, there for just such an emergency. Smoke billowed out, followed by the Marines. Johnson and Duncan handed an injured man, Mead, down from the top of the track, and then they jumped down to try to gather their squads and help with the casualties. They both raced to the rear of C211. One Marine had nearly lost his leg, and his fellow Marines were ordered to get him to the corpsmen as quickly as possible. The Marines scooped up the casualties and carried them down off the road, out of the line of enemy fire.

Duncan and Johnson grabbed a wounded Marine and, dodging the bullets that were slapping against the side of the burning track, ran down the side of the raised road and plopped their load on the ground at a hastily arranged aid station. Corpsmen began working on the Marine immediately. In addition to Mead and Glass, there were two more wounded Marines. One had a severe leg wound and a Gunny had been temporarily blinded.

As the corpsmen were tending to the wounded, Lt. Seely was deploying his Marines. He sent several to the berm east of the road, and he ordered the rest to follow him to the western side of the road. The road was raised above the surrounding terrain and the enemy was sweeping the road with machine gun and small-arms fire. Seely went first, not knowing how many of his men would follow. All ten of the Marines followed their platoon leader across the elevated road to the western side. The Marines dove for cover in a water-filled ditch along the side of the road. Suddenly, a Marine splashed down almost on top of Seely. It was Sgt. Bitz, face to face with Seely, still wearing his AMTRAC crew helmet and carrying his M16. He smiled at Seely, "It looks like I'm a Grunt now, Sir."

As Seely's Marines were racing across the road, enemy mortar rounds began to fall, first in the distance, then closer with each volley. The Iraqis were pounding Charlie Company with everything they had – artillery, mortars, RPGs, machine guns and small-arms fire from both sides of the road and south of the canal.

The Iraqi 11th Infantry Division commander had expected an American airborne assault into the open fields northeast of the city. So, he had positioned his troops and indirect fire assets so that they were zeroed in on the 1km-long (0.6 miles) elevated road north of the Saddam Canal. Charlie Company had stopped right in the middle of the Iraqi commander's fire sack.

Duncan and Johnson dived across Mead and Glass when they heard the mortar rounds whistling in, shielding the wounded Marines. Meanwhile, the FiST had set up his three 60mm mortars nearby. Charlie Company's mortar teams were in a deadly duel with the Iraqis. After several minutes, the Iraqis zeroed in on one of the Marine's mortars. Another mortar round came whistling in, Duncan and Johnson shielded their charges again, and Johnson watched as the round landed amid the Marine mortar team.

The Weapons Platoon Leader, 1st Lt. James Reid, and the FO were both thrown in the air, three Marines lay dead, and another four were wounded. Amazingly, Reid was still alive. He looked around and saw the dead and wounded Marines, rose to his feet, and sprinted toward Duncan, Johnson and the corpsmen to get help for his men. Another round landed not ten feet in front of him. It knocked him to the ground again. He rose again. His face had been peppered with shrapnel and one of his eyes was badly injured. He thought that he had lost his eye. Reid ran to his mortar track and asked a Gunny. "How is my eye? Is it gone?" Then the Gunny carefully inspected the wound. "You are good to go, Sir." Reid turned to the men in the track and ordered them to help the wounded. "If I don't come back, load them up and get them south to safety, no matter how much it hurts." Then Reid turned and ran to find his company commander.

By now, Sgt. Schafer, with Duncan and Johnson's help, was loading the wounded and dead Marines into C201, C206, and C208. Schafer, unable to contact any of his officers, was considering leading the three tracks back through Ambush Alley to get the wounded to safety. There was no way anyone could bring a helicopter into this firefight. Driving the wounded south was the only way to get them help.

Charlie Company was still taking heavy fire. Even some of the wounded were returning fire with their rifles. Schafer immediately ordered the three

tracks to button up and move out. Duncan and Johnson jumped into C206. Johnson wanted to check to make sure everyone was aboard. "Hold the ramp. Let me take one last look." Then he jumped out for a sweep of the area.

A mortar round screamed in and Johnson went down. C206's driver had already begun to roll forward. One of the passengers yelled for the driver to halt, but by the time they had stopped, Johnson was lying in a heap nearly 100 meters from the vehicle.

Duncan sprinted to his friend, pulled him up into a fireman's carry and ran back toward C206. By the time Duncan reached the track, he was spent. He gently lowered Johnson onto the floor of the track, shouted for the corpsman, and then he collapsed. C206's driver gunned the engine and raced south over the Saddam Canal. Schafer had stopped all three tracks when Johnson was hit. Now C206 led the medevac column south. C208 followed C206, and C201 was the last track up onto the bridge.

The lead track was just coming down off the bridge when a thunderous explosion erupted between C206 and C208. The roof of C206 caved in and its back ramp crashed open, but the track kept rolling forward. Seconds later C208 received a direct hit, blowing the vehicle nearly in half. C201 lost its steering and ran into a telephone pole. All the Marines in C201 poured out into a house along the side of the road. Meanwhile, the driver and track commander of C208 climbed out of their mangled track, both wounded but miraculously still alive. The Marines in the troop compartment never knew what had hit them.

The two wounded trackers limped to the house with the other Marines. They took refuge there until they could be rescued. C206 continued south through Ambush Alley. By the time they reached Alpha Company's position at the Euphrates River, the rest of Grabowski's tanks had arrived. C206 rolled into Alpha Company's position and a RPG

ABOVE **1st Sgt. Jose Henao of Charlie Company, 1st Battalion, 2d Marines, inspects the burned-out hulk of C211, the first AMTRAC hit in Ambush Alley. (Courtesy of David Dunfee USMC)**

screamed out of a building. It hit the side of the track, rocking it furiously. A second RPG shot through the air and went in through the back opening. The explosion stopped the vehicle dead in its tracks.

Alpha Company Marines ran to the crippled track. The first Marine there found a pile of twisted metal. He couldn't believe it when he heard a groan. Two Marines were buried in the pile of debris with the center beam of the troop compartment roof covering them. One of the Marine's helmets was nearly crushed under the weight of the heavy metal support and he was pinned at the head, but he was alive. The Marines began to carefully try to extract him. "Any aircraft, any aircraft! This is 'Kool Aide' on TAD. I have immediate need for med-evac in Nasiriyah." Alpha Company's FAC broadcast over and over until he got a response. His call for help was relayed to the regimental headquarters where two "Phrogs" were waiting on standby for just this sort of mission.

Capt. Eric Garcia ran to his waiting CH-46 with his crew and took to the skies. They headed north. "Kool Aide, this is Parole-Two-Five inbound on med-evac," Garcia announced to the FAC on the ground. "Parole-Two-Five, we are just north of the Euphrates River Bridge. The area is as secure as we can make it, but we are taking fire. The LZ is HOT." Without hesitation, Garcia responded, "Roger, Kool Aide." He ordered Parole-Two-Six to stand off and not to land. Then, Garcia followed his gunship escorts across the Euphrates River and set down right in the middle of Alpha Company's raging firefight. He waited as Duncan was carefully removed from the wreckage and quickly rushed to the back of the waiting med-evac helicopter. Marines rushed him into the Phrog and struggled to lay him on one of the litters mounted on the walls of the helicopter. "Put him down. Put him down," the crew chief

ABOVE **A Humvee or HMMWV from Task Force Tarawa and MAG-29 Phrog alongside Route Moe, just south of An Nasiriyah, March 23, 2003. (Courtesy of Kevin Ellicot USMC)**

commanded. The unconscious Marine was laid out on the deck. Garcia raced the engines and lifted back into the air once he heard the crew chief shout, "Go! Go! Go!" Within seconds, Parole-Two-Five was back out over the Iraqi desert and flying toward a field hospital in Kuwait.

Back at C206, Johnson, who had been pinned under Duncan, was dazed but uninjured. He climbed from the wreckage and was moved into a building where the less seriously wounded casualties were being housed.

AFTER THE BATTLE

Just after Garcia's helicopter lifted into the blue sky, Capt. Brooks ordered his men to mount up. Alpha Company pushed forward through Ambush Alley to reinforce Charlie Company, north of the canal. Bravo Company met Alpha in the center of Ambush Alley and they, too, moved across the bridge. As the sun set, all of the Timberwolves were north of the Saddam Canal, guarding the northern bridge. "America's Battalion" moved in behind 1/2 and they secured the Euphrates River Bridge.

Med-evac

During the flight Duncan moved in and out of consciousness. He had no idea where he was. There were two Marines huddled over him. He could hear them talking but he was missing most of the words. The two men working intently to stabilize Duncan were actually Navy corpsmen. They inserted IV drips, administered morphine, and continued to monitor Duncan's vital signs as Garcia raced south. Duncan drifted back into semi-consciousness again and felt the chopper gently touching down. He thought that this had to be the smoothest landing he had ever experienced in one of these warhorses. In an instant, the familiar corpsmen were at his side and others were carrying his litter from the helicopter. He was rushed toward a MASH unit tent.

RIGHT **US Marines care for their casualties at the 2d Battalion, 8th Marines Battalion Aid Station, south of An Nasiriyah, on March 24, 2003. The modern-day Marine Corps boasts excellent medical care that saves the lives of many Marines who would not have been so lucky in previous wars. (Courtesy of Kevin Ellicot USMC)**

Halfway there, the Marines were met by a group of army medics and nurses. They quickly took the litter and rushed Duncan inside. Duncan felt a rush of cool air. It was the first air-conditioned air he had felt since leaving the ship. He was hoisted onto an operating table. The lights were brighter than the sun. He only had an instant to see a gang of surgeons and scrub nurses descend upon him. They were cutting off his clothes. Duncan was out cold, knocked out by the anaesthetist.

In any other war, a wounded Marine like Duncan never would have survived his life-threatening injury. Today, a heroic pilot and his flight crew had literally yanked him from the jaws of death. Navy corpsmen had administered life-saving first aid as the air ambulance raced south. Duncan was brought to a field hospital that would rival any hospital emergency room in the world. He was immediately diagnosed and stabilized. Then he was loaded onto another helicopter and flown to the giant white hospital ship, USS *Comfort*, at anchor in the Persian Gulf. Duncan remained unconscious, never even knowing that he had been flown out of the war zone.

Three days after drifting off on the Kuwaiti operating table, Duncan awoke with three-quarters of his face bandaged. He was in the giant American medical facility in Landstul, Germany. The hospital director, Col. (Dr.) Ronda Cornum, checked on Duncan as soon as she heard that he had regained consciousness. She had a special interest in all of the young casualties, having survived a Black Hawk helicopter crash in Iraq during *Desert Storm*, only to be captured and held prisoner for nearly a week. Col. Cornum spent nearly 30 minutes at Duncan's bedside, telling him about his injuries and what the medical staff had done to save his life. Duncan didn't spend much time at Landstul. The next morning he was loaded onto an air force bus outfitted to carry litters. Duncan was the first patient carried aboard. Covered in bandages and still in a neck brace, he could only see a small reading lamp above his head. The second man aboard the bus was placed right across the aisle from Duncan. He quickly discovered that this man was Lt. Reid.

The fight for Baghdad

Meanwhile, the Marines of the RCT-1 began moving through Ambush Alley on the day after RCT-2's bloody battle for the eastern bridges, and RCT-5 and RCT-7 pushed north across the far western bridge that 3/2 had secured the previous day. LtCol. Eddie Ray's 2d Light Armored Reconnaissance Battalion crossed the eastern bridges, shot past Johnson and the Timberwolves, and then up Highway 7 toward Baghdad as RCT-5 led the charge up Highway 8. Ray's LAVs did not get very far before they became heavily engaged with Iraqi forces that were moving south to reinforce the beleaguered fighters in An Nasiriyah. 2d LAR's heavily armed Light Armored Vehicles decimated the Iraqis before they even got within firing range of the American Marines.

RCT-1 waited until after nightfall on the 24th to charge through Ambush Alley and didn't catch up with LtCol. Ray's Marines until the morning of the 25th. The Marines of the 1st Marine Division charged north on a two-pronged attack until a massive sandstorm stopped the American advance in its tracks. On the afternoon of the 25th, the storm morphed into torrential rains, thunder, and lightning.

American military commanders took this opportunity to re-supply the forward combat units. After the bloody battle for An Nasiriyah, the news media reported that the invasion was "bogging down." But once the weather had cleared and the forward units had been re-supplied, the Army and Marines rolled forward again.

After the experiences in An Nasiriyah, commanders in the 1st Marine Division tried hard to avoid major Iraqi population centers. RCT-5 and RCT-7 charged up Highway 8 past Ad Diwaniyah, while RCT-1 advanced up Highway 7 to Al Kut. RCT-5 and RCT-7 moved back to the east and rejoined RCT-1 at the Iraqi town of Sabat. From there, the entire division pushed north for the last 161km (100 miles) on the eastern road into Baghdad.

The 1st Marine Division encountered ever-increasing resistance as they moved closer to Saddam's center of power. By the time the Marines reached Baghdad, the Iraqi leadership was on the run. They moved into

LEFT **Marines from the 1st Battalion, 2d Marine Regiment, clear a small village near the southern Iraqi city of An Nasiriyah. (Courtesy of Joe Raedle/Getty Images)**

the center of Baghdad and skirted the eastern side of the city, all the while encountering pockets of resistance. Within days, the Marines had silenced organized enemy resistance in the capital.

Meanwhile, Johnson and the rest of 1/2 spent the last week of March setting up checkpoints and road blocks, north of An Nasiriyah. They continued to expand their security perimeter until it engulfed all the roads and bridges leading into An Nasiriyah from the north. An Nasiriyah remained surrounded as the rest of RCT-2 worked to clear the southern part of the city of the remaining Ba'ath Party and Fedayeen holdouts. As Task Force Tarawa worked to secure the city, convoy after convoy rolled through Ambush Alley and over the bridges that the Timberwolves had fought so hard to secure.

After a week of fighting, Task Force Tarawa defeated Saddam's Fedayeen fighters in and around An Nasiriyah. Natonski's Brigade was reinforced with two MEUs. Once reinforced, Task Force Tarawa moved north and fanned out to secure most of southern Iraq. Major combat operations were over for the Marines of Task Force Tarawa but the next couple of months would be filled with some small skirmishes and security and stabilization operations. By April 7, the Marines of 1st Division were at the gates of Baghdad. There were several days of intense fighting but the Iraqi fighters quickly melted away into the civilian population. The war had been won, but winning the peace would prove to be much more difficult.

Task Force Tarawa patrolled the streets of the towns of the Fertile Crescent. They met with local officials, handed out food and water, and started rebuilding Iraq. The Marines turned from conquest to relief operations. They provided medical care for the people; they repaired electrical networks and water pumping stations. They rebuilt bridges, schools, and mosques. Most importantly, they maintained order and started to aid the local population in rebuilding their lives in a democracy. The MEB staff began measuring success by the number of Iraqi children returning to school.

RIGHT **An Iraqi boy on the outskirts of An Nasiriyah. (Photo courtesy Capt. Harold Qualkinbush USMC)**

Camp Lejeune's Marines were moved back to Kuwait and loaded onto their ATF-E ships by May 18 for their month-long journey home. In a short six months, they had traveled halfway around the world to fight the first major battle of Operation *Iraqi Freedom*; they had brought a new stability to southern Iraq, and returned to their families in North Carolina. Saddam Hussein had been defeated but the war still raged. Some of Task Force Tarawa's Marines would return to civilian life, but most would return to Iraq in the months to come.

ABOVE **A peaceful crowd of Iraqi civilians meet 2d Battalion, 8th Division Marines in Al Kut. After several tense moments the crowd dispersed with no incident. After the fighting was over, ordinary Marines faced perhaps greater challenges during the stabilization operations as they worked to win the support of the local population. Note also the press figure with camera standing amongst the Marines. Operation *Iraqi Freedom* attracted constant controversy and media attention. (Courtesy of Kevin Ellicot USMC)**

LEFT **Marines in An Nasiriyah help distribute flour to hungry civilians. The supplies had been stockpiled by the Iraqi military. (Courtesy of Joe Raedle/Getty Images)**

GLOSSARY

81s	81mm Mortar Platoon		**IFF**	Identification-Friend or Foe
AAV	Assault Amphibian Vehicle		**I MEF**	1st Marine Expeditionary Forces
ACE	Aviation Combat Element (USMC)		**IS**	Immediate Suppression
AMTRAC	Amphibious Tracked Vehicle (AAV)		**KIA**	Killed In Action
AO	Air Officer		**LAAD**	Light Anti-Aircraft Defense system, mounted
ARG	Amphibious Ready Group			on HMMWV
ATF-E	Amphibious Task Force – East ("the		**LAR**	Light Armored Reconnaissance
	Magnificent Seven")		**LAV**	Light Armored Vehicle
ATO	Air Tasking Order		**LAV-25**	Light Armored Vehicle with 25mm
AVLB	Armored Vehicle Launched Bridges			Bushmaster automatic cannon
BAS	Battalion Aid Station		**LAV-AT**	Light Armored Vehicle – Anti-tank – TOW
BDA	Battle Damage Assessment			missile launcher
BDRM	Soviet wheeled armored reconnaissance		**LCAC**	Landing Craft Air Cushioned
	vehicle		**LCU**	Landing Craft Utility
BDU	Battle Dress Uniform		**LHA**	Landing Helicopter Assault (Ship)
BMP	Russian-built tracked, armored personnel		**LHD**	Landing Helicopter Dock (Ship)
	carrier		**LNO**	Liaison Officer
BTR-60	Soviet-made wheeled infantry vehicle		**LOD**	Line of Departure
C3	Command, Control, and Communications		**LPD**	Landing Platform Dock (Ship)
CAAT	Combined Anti-Armor Team		**LSD**	Landing Supply Dock (Ship)
CAG	Civil Action Group – interpreters		**LVS**	Four-wheel drive heavy lift vehicle
CAS	Close Air Support		**LZ**	Landing Zone
CAX	Combined Arms Exercise		**MAG**	Marine Air Group
CENTCOM	US Central Command		**MAGTF**	Marine Air Ground Task Force
CFF	Call For Fire		**MAW**	Marine Air Wing
CFLCC	Combined Force Land Component		**MCAGCC**	Marine Corps Air Ground Combat Center
	Commander			(Twentynine Palms, Ca.)
Chop	Removing unit from its parent and assigning		**MEB**	Marine Expeditionary Brigade
	it to another unit		**MEF**	Marine Expeditionary Force
COC	Command Operations Center		**MEU (SOC)**	Marine Expeditionary Unit (Special
comms	Communications			Operations Capable)
CP	Command Post		**MK148**	Four Pack HMMWV containing a high
CSSA	Combined Services and Support Area			power radio
DI	Drill Instructor		**MLRS**	Multiple Launch Rocket System
EAAK	External Appliqué Armor Kit (for AAVs)		**MOPP**	Mission Oriented Protective Posture
EPW	Enemy Prisoner of War		**MOS**	Military Occupational Specialty
FAC	Forward Air Controller		**MOUT**	Military Operations in Urban Terrain
FARP	Forward Area Resupply Point		**MRE**	Meal-Ready-to-Eat
FAST	Forward Area Support Team		**MSR**	Main Supply Route
FINEX	Final Exercise		**MTLB**	Soviet armored, amphibious, multi-purpose
FiST	Fire Support Team			personnel carrier
FLOT	Forward Line of Troops		**NATO**	North Atlantic Treaty Organization
FO	Forward Observer		**NBC**	Nuclear, Biological, and Chemical
FOB	Forward Operating Base		**NCO**	Non-Commissioned Officer
FROG	Free Rocket over Ground – Russian-built		**NVGs**	Night Vision Goggles
	artillery rocket		**Phrogs**	Marine nickname for Sea Knight CH-46
FSB	Forward Support Battalion			helicopter
FSC	Fire Support Coordinator		**PL**	Phase Line
GCE	Ground Combat Element		**POW**	Prisoner of War
GP	General Purpose		**PT**	Physical Training
GPS	Global Positioning System		**RAP**	Rocket-Assisted Projectile
HE	High Explosive		**RCT**	Regimental Combat Team
HEAT	High Explosive Anti Tank		**RGFC**	Republican Guard Forces Command
HEMTT	Heavy Expanded Mobility Tactical Truck		**RIP**	Relief in Place
HET	Heavy Equipment Transporter		**ROC**	Rehearsal of Concept
HHC	Headquarters and Headquarters Company		**ROE**	Rules of Engagement
HMMWV	High Mobility Multi-Wheeled Vehicle		**RORO**	Roll-On, Roll-Off – military cargo ships have
IFAV	Infantry Fast Attack Vehicle			RORO capability

RPG	Rocket-Propelled Grenade			(platoon/team) snipers
RPV	Remote-Piloted Vehicle	**TAA**	Tactical Assembly Area
RRP	Rapid Re-supply Point	**TCP**	Tactical Control Point
SA-2	Russian-built Surface-to-Air missile	**TEWT**	Tactical Exercise Without Troops
SAM	Surface-to-Air Missile	**TF**	Task Force
SAW	Squad Automatic Weapon	**TFS**	Tactical Fighter Squadron
SCUD	Russian Ballistic missile	**TOC**	Tactical Operations Center
Seabees	US Navy Construction Battalion	**TOW**	Tube-launched, Optically-tracked, Wire-
SEAD	Suppression of Enemy Air Defenses		guided, antitank missile
SEAL	Sea, Air, and Land – US Navy's elite	**TRAP**	Tactical Recovery – Aircraft and Personnel
	commando unit.	**UAV**	Unmanned Aerial Vehicle
SF	Special Forces	**USMC**	United States Marine Corps
Skids	Marine nickname for Cobras and Hueys	**USNS**	United States Naval Ship – ships of the
Snake	Marine nickname for a Cobra helicopter		military sealift command
SOC	Special Operations Capable – USMC as in	**USS**	United States Ship
	MEU (SOC)	**VTOL**	Vertical Take Off and Landing
SOI	School of Infantry	**WSO**	Weapon Systems Officer – WSO in
SOS	Special Operations Squadron – USAF		backseat of Air Force jets
STA	Surveillance and Target Acquisition	**ZSU23-4**	Radar-guided Anti-Aircraft-Artillery

BIBLIOGRAPHY

Anderson, Jon Lee, *The Fall of Baghdad*, Penguin Press, New York, 2004

Clancy, Tom, *Marine – A Guided Tour of a Marine Expeditionary Unit*, Berkley, New York, 1996

Lowry, Richard S., *Marines in the Garden of Eden*, Berkley, New York, 2006

Murray, Williamson, and Robert Scales, *The Iraq War: A Military History*, Harvard University Press, Cambridge, 2003

Pollack, Kenneth, *The Threatening Storm*, Random House, New York, 2002

Rick, Thomas, *Making the Corps*, Scribner, New York, 1998

Roux, Georges, *Ancient Iraq*, Penguin Books (3rd ed.), London, 1992

Stockman, James R. Capt. (USMC), *Marines in World War II Historical Monograph – The Battle for Tarawa*, Historical Section, Division of Public Information Headquarters, US Marine Corps, 1947

Trewhitt, Philip, *Armored Fighting Vehicles – 300 of the world's greatest military vehicles*, Barnes & Noble Books, New York, 1999

West, Bing and Ray L. Major General USMC (Ret.) Smith, *The March Up*, Bantam Books, New York, 2003

COLOR PLATE COMMENTARY

A: TASK FORCE TARAWA MARINE

From their lightweight waterproof boots to their Kevlar helmets, Marine infantrymen were some of the best-equipped war fighters in the world. Their clothing was made of the most advanced materials, designed to be light, yet durable. The camouflage patterns on their outer garments were scientifically developed to provide maximum cover in either wooded or desert environments.

Here our composite character, Cpl. Terrell Johnson, can be seen dressed to fight on any battlefield. He is carrying the standard M16A2 rifle, equipped with a M203 grenade launcher. He has standard-issue goggles, which were an absolute necessity during desert sandstorms.

Johnson is wearing his MOPP suit pants and jumper which provide protection against nuclear, biological, and chemical attacks. The Marines trained continually at donning the rest of their protective clothing: mask, hood, heavy rubber gloves, and booties which were all carried in a pouch strapped to their upper thigh. Every Marine was issued a Kevlar helmet and flak vest to protect their head and torso from small-arms fire and shrapnel, and they were given knee pads and gloves to protect their knees and hands from minor injuries.

Task Force Tarawa Marines were all issued Marine desert camouflage utility uniforms which included a desert camouflage helmet cover, but they received MOPP suits in woodland camouflage. MOPP suits are stored in airtight packaging and will become ineffective after a few days of exposure to the atmosphere. Most MOPP suits were manufactured to provide protection to American servicemen in a potential war with the former Soviet Union. A war with the Soviet Union would most certainly have been fought in the forests of Europe, so it made sense to use woodland patterns for the MOPP suits. These suits had been sitting on supply shelves, collecting dust, since the fall of the Soviet Union. Now, the suits were needed and commanders decided to provide the protective garments to all of the troops even though they were green. This strange combination of desert and woodland camouflage gave Task Force Tarawa Marines a unique look.

1. M249 Squad Automatic Weapon uses the same Standard NATO 5.56mm ammunition as the M16A2 rifle
2a. Standard NATO 5.56mm ball round
2b. Standard NATO 5.56mm tracer round
3a. Mk113 gas mask
3b. MOPP suit protective hood
4a. Woodland camouflage pattern of MOPP hooded jacket
4b. Gas mask pouch
4c. Knee pads
4d. Desert boots
5. Web belt with canteen and ammunition pouches
6. Back pack and camelback (only drinking tube is visible)
7. Flak vest

B: RECRUIT TRAINING

At Parris Island, South Carolina and at the Marine Corps Recruit Depot, San Diego, California, teenagers are turned into Marines. The transformation is complete in body, mind, and spirit. The moment these young men step off the bus and onto the painted yellow footprints on the pavement beneath them, they are molded and shaped. All vestiges of their past life are taken away, including their hair. Then, they are rebuilt in the Marine Corps mold. By the end of their training, they move together as one. They think and act alike. They become Marines.

C: COMBINED ARMS EXERCISE

This is where the Marines put it all together. Fixed and rotary wing air support, lift helicopter crews, Combined Anti-Armor Teams (CAAT), Amphibious Armored Vehicles (AAVs), M1A1 Abrams tanks, mortars, artillery, and logistic support are all combined in support of Marine infantry. During this training, the Marines become an integrated Marine Air Ground Task Force (MAGTF), a combined arms team unequaled in the world.

Seen here are infantrymen dismounting from their AAVP7 AMTRAC amphibious tractor as an M1A1 Abrams tank, a CAAT TOW gunner and an AH-1 COBRA gunship provide supporting fire in the sandy southern California desert. The Marine Corps Air, Ground Combat Center (MCAGCC) at Twentynine Palms, California, is one of the few training facilities large enough to support regimental-level, combined arms, live-fire exercises.

ABOVE **Homemade mileage signposts dotted Camp Shoup in the Kuwaiti desert. This particular signpost was constructed by Marines of the 2d Regiment's Intelligence shop. (Courtesy of Joe Muccia USMC)**

D: AN NASIRIYAH

The fighting began along Route Moe at an uncharted railroad overpass near the Euphrates River when the Marines encountered a dug-in Iraqi tank company supported by mortars and infantry. The Forward Air Controllers (FACs) of 1/2 Marines immediately called for close air support and Marine Cobras swooped in.

Just as they had practiced at Combined Arms Exercise in Twentynine Palms, CAAT TOW gunners methodically fired on dug-in Iraqi tanks, while the Cobra gunships overhead fired on anything that moved. Cobras provide the Marines with extensive airborne close air support capabilities. The Gatling gun can lay down massive amounts of directed fire on the enemy. Cobras can also carry extremely accurate Hellfire antitank missiles and Hydra rocket pods, which can fill an area the size of a football field with deadly fire in a single salvo.

E: CAMP SHOUP

Task Force Tarawa's Marines carved a home out of the northern Kuwaiti desert wasteland, waiting for the order to move into Iraq. Camp Shoup (named after Col. David M. Shoup, the 2d Marine Regiment's commanding officer at the battle of Tarawa, Medal of Honor winner and eventual commandant of the Marine Corps), housed the modern-day Regimental Combat Team-2 (RCT-2) within its berms.

Everyday life for the Marines in Kuwait was Spartan at best. The availability of electricity was limited. The Marines slept on the sand floors of their tents and washed themselves and their clothes in cold water. The desert sand invaded everything on good days, and weekly sandstorms filled the sky, browning out the sun. The larger storms pulled tent pegs from the ground, toppling tents and scattering everything that wasn't nailed down.

The Marines' days were filled with waiting. They read books, magazines, and old newspapers, and wrote letters home. They made makeshift road signs which displayed how far it was to their home. Their boredom was interspersed with training, drills, PT, and constant cleaning of their weapons and equipment. Even in the barren desert, out of the view of anyone but themselves, they proudly displayed the crimson and gold United States Marine Corps' flag.

F: MED-EVAC

Casualties were moved to safety and life-saving medical attention faster in Operation *Iraqi Freedom* than in any other war in history. Heroic pilots and their CH-46 crews landed in hot landing zones (LZs) while the fighting still raged to whisk their charges to state-of-the-art medical facilities which rivaled any major metropolitan emergency room, saving many Marine lives.

Here, Capt. Eric Garcia lands along Highway 7, north of the Saddam Canal, in the midst of 1st Battalion, 2d Marines' battle on March 23, 2003. Capt. Garcia returned to the battlefield, landing three times in all. Each time he and his crew whisked wounded Timberwolves to safety and vital medical attention. He saved more than one Marine's life that day, earning the Distinguished Flying Cross for his selfless actions under enemy fire.

The CH-46 "Sea Knight" helicopter has been in service in the United States Marine Corps since the Vietnam War. It is a workhorse used for many different missions. It can lift 25 fully equipped Marines into battle and can be used to ferry supplies to Marines on the battlefield. One of the "Phrogs" most important capabilities is its ability to be configured as an airborne ambulance.

G: MARINES ON PARADE

The dress blue uniform of the United States Marine Corps is unique and filled with tradition. It is made from the colors of the US flag – red, white and blue. Each button bares the Eagle, Globe, and Anchor insignia, the oldest American military insignia in continued use.

The scarlet stripe or "blood stripe" that runs down each trouser leg of commissioned and non-commissioned officers originally honored the Marines who had fallen in the "Halls of Montezuma", during the 1846–48 Mexican War. Today, the stripes honor all of the Marines who have fallen throughout history, defending freedom and democracy. The high-neck collar is a remnant from the American Revolution when Marines wore leather stock to protect their necks from sword blows during ship boardings, earning them the nickname of "leathernecks." The uniform can be worn in several configurations depending on the occasion; Blue Dress A (with medals), Blue Dress B (with ribbons), Blue Dress C (sky blue trousers with khaki shirt, field scarf and ribbons), and Blue Dress C (short sleeved khaki shirt and ribbons).

Marine officers have carried the Mameluke Sword since 1804, when Lt. Presley O'Bannon was presented with one by Hamet Karamanli after his victory at Tripoli during the Barbary Wars. The sword is a replica of those carried by Karamanli's Mameluke tribesmen and to this day commemorates the Corps' first victory on foreign soil.

BELOW **Camp Shoup during a minor sandstorm.**
(Photo courtesy Capt. Harold Qualkinbush USMC)

INDEX

References to illustrations are shown in **bold**. Plates are shown with page and caption locators in brackets.